Viva fastrack

MATHS

BOOK 3

Jeff Geha

Viva Books Private Limited
New Delhi • Mumbai • Chennai • Kolkata • Bangalore • Hyderabad

First Indian Edition 2007

VIVA BOOKS PRIVATE LIMITED

- 4737/23 Ansari Road, Daryaganj, New Delhi 110 002
  E-mail: vivadelhi@vivagroupindia.net, Tel. 42242200
- Plot No. 76, Service Industries, Shirvane, Sector 1, Nerul, Navi Mumbai 400 706
  E-mail: vivamumbai@vivagroupindia.net, Tel. 27721273, 27721274
- Jamals Fazal Chambers, 26 Greams Road, Chennai 600 006
  E-mail: vivachennai@vivagroupindia.net, Tel. 28290304, 28294241
- B-103, Jindal Towers, 21/1A/3 Darga Road, Kolkata 700 017
  E-mail: vivakolkata@vivagroupindia.net, Tel. 22836381, 22816713
- 7, Sovereign Park Apartments, 56-58, K. R. Road, Basavanagudi, Bangalore 560 004
  E-mail: vivabangalore@vivagroupindia.net, Tel. 26607409, 26607410
- 101-102 Mughal Marc Apartments, 3-4-637 to 641, Narayanguda, Hyderabad 500 029
  E-mail: vivahyderabad@vivagroupindia.net, Tel. 27564481, 27564482

Published by arrangement with

Pascal Educational Services
655 Parramatta Road
Leichhardt, NSW 2040
Australia

ISBN 81-7649-623-5

Published by Vinod Vasishtha for Viva Books Private Limited, 4737/23, Ansari Road, New Delhi 110 002. Printed and bound at Anand Sons, Delhi.

CONTENTS

INTRODUCTION

This intermediate mathematics Pocket Book was conceived after countless suggestions made by students to have a comprehensive, easy to follow guide that covers all aspects of the syllabus.

The Years 9 & 10 Intermediate book gives students step-by-step methods to solve all maths problems, with valuable commentary and advice. It contains 'All You Need To Know', so any student with full knowledge of this pocket book should be well prepared for Years 9 & 10 Intermediate maths exams.

ABOUT THE AUTHOR

Jeff Geha is an Actuary and international mathematics author with over 20 books published to date. He has been tutoring students for over 10 years and his unique approach to teaching mathematics has received considerable media attention. He is one of the principal founders of HSC Fast Track, a leading HSC tuition school.

CHAPTER 1: NUMBER REVIEW AND APPROXIMATIONS

This topic is a revision of the concepts covered in Year 8.

Students should be reminded to follow these steps, when rounding off answers to problems:

> 1 Write down initial calculator display in full before rounding off.
>
> 2 **Decimal figures** begin with the *first digit after the decimal point.*
>
> 3 **Significant figures** begin with the *first non-zero digit.*
>
> 4 **Rounding off:**
> If the next digit is $\geqslant 5$, then round up.
> If the next digit is < 5, then round down.

Note: The calculator can be used to give answers correct to ***n*** decimal places or significant figures as follows:

Decimal Places:	MODE	7	*n*
Significant Figures:	MODE	8	*n*

This gives the result in scientific notation (refer to page 19, for details) then you simply expand it to get into significant figures.

'*n*' is the number of decimal places or significant figures asked in the question.

CHAPTER 2: RATES AND SCALE DRAWINGS

This topic is also part of the Year 8 course. Below is a summary of the important formulae:

Speed, Time, Distance

$$\text{Speed (S)} = \frac{\text{Distance}}{\text{Time}} = \frac{D}{T}$$

$$\text{Time (T)} = \frac{\text{Distance}}{\text{Speed}} = \frac{D}{S}$$

$$\text{Distance (D)} = \text{Speed} \times \text{Time} = S \times T$$

Scale Drawings

The ratio of a scale drawing to the original is called the scale.

Scale = length on drawing : real length

A EARNING MONEY

i Salary

A salary is a fixed amount of money earned per year, which is paid on a regular basis – weekly, fortnightly or monthly.

The following conversions should be known:

1 year = 52 weeks

1 year = 26 fortnights

1 fortnight = 2 weeks

ii Wages and Overtime

A wage is a variable amount of money earned per week. It is based on the number of hours worked for the week, the normal hourly rate and the number of hours worked overtime.

Overtime rates are paid for hours worked outside the normal working day. The rate for overtime hours is called 'time and a half' (1.5 × normal rate) and 'double time' (2 × normal rate).

In summary, a wage is made up of 3 components:

1. Normal wage
   = normal rate $\times$ regular hours
2. Time and a half
   = normal rate $\times$ 1.5 $\times$ overtime hours
3. Double time
   = normal rate $\times$ 2 $\times$ overtime hours

EXAMPLE

Craig works as a waiter. During a week, he worked 38 normal hours, 4 hours at time and a half and 5 hours at double time.

Find Craig's weekly wage if he earns $14.00 per hour.

SOLUTION

Craig's wage is made up of 3 components:

1 Normal wage = normal rate × regular hours
= \$14.00 × 38
= \$532

2 Time and a half
= normal rate × 1.5 × overtime hours
= \$14.00 × 1.5 × 4
= \$84

3 Double time = normal rate × 2 × overtime hours
= \$14.00 × 2 × 5
= \$140

∴ Craig's weekly wage = 532 + 84 + 140
= \$756

iii Commission

There are many persons in the workforce who are paid a commission when they sell an item (eg car salesman, real estate agents etc.).

The commission is expressed as a percentage of the value of the goods sold.

EXAMPLE

A real estate agent charges 4% commission for the first \$50 000 of the value of the house and 2.5% thereafter. Calculate the commission the agent will earn on a unit worth \$195 000.

SOLUTION

Balance over \$50 000 = \$195 000 – 50 000
= \$145 000

Agent's commission
= (5% × \$50 000) + (2.5% × \$145 000)
= 0.05 × 50 000 + 0.025 × \$145 000
= 2500 + 3625
= \$6125

∴ The agent receives a \$6125 commission for selling the unit.

iv Income Tax

Income tax is calculated on a person's 'taxable income'.

Taxable Income
= Gross Income – Allowable Deductions

To find the tax paid on a person's 'taxable income' a tax table is used.

EXAMPLE

Susan's gross income was $38 000. Her total allowable deductions were $2500.

Find the tax she must pay using the tax table below.

TAXABLE INCOME	TAX
$1 – $5400	Nil
$5401 – $20700	Nil plus 20 c for each $ over $5400
$20701 – $36 000	$3060 plus 38 c for each $ over $20 700
$36001 – $50000	$8874 plus 46 c for each $ over $36 000
$50 001 and over	$15 314 plus 47 c for each $ over $50 000

SOLUTION

Taxable Income
= Gross Income – Allowable Deductions
= \$38 000 – \$2500
= \$35 500

From the table \$35 500 falls in the tax bracket \$20 701 – \$36 000.

∴ Tax payable = \$3060 + 38 c for each \$ over \$20 700
= \$3060 + \$0.38 × (\$35 500 – \$20 700)
= \$3060 + \$0.38 × 14 800
= \$3060 + \$5624
= \$8684

∴ Susan must pay \$8684 in tax.

B SPENDING MONEY

i Simple Interest

The interest earned when investing (or borrowing) at a simple (or flat) rate is given by:

$$I = \frac{P \times R \times N}{100}$$

where:

I = Simple interest

P = Principal borrowed/invested

R = Rate of interest as a %

N = Number of years

EXAMPLE

Find the simple interest earned if Emma invests $5000 at 5% p.a. for 2 years.

SOLUTION

$$I = \frac{P \times R \times N}{100} \qquad P = 5000, R = 5, N = 2$$

$$= \frac{5000 \times 5 \times 2}{100} = \$500$$

ii Loan Repayments

This is a common application involving the simple interest formula.

EXAMPLE

Derek borrows \$4000 from a bank to buy an entertainment unit. He is required to repay the loan, plus simple interest at 8.5% p.a., over 3 years.

Find:

i How much money Derek has to pay to the bank over the 3 years.

ii The value of each instalment, if Derek paid the loan in quarterly instalments over the 3 year period.

SOLUTION

i Interest paid on the loan is given by:

$$I = \frac{P \times R \times N}{100} \qquad P = 4000,\ R = 8.5,\ N = 3$$

$$= \frac{4000 \times 8.5 \times 3}{100} = \$1020$$

∴ Total amount paid by Derek
= \$4000 + \$1020
= \$5020

ii Number of quarterly payments in 1 year = 4
Number of quarterly payments in 3 years = 12

$$\therefore \text{Quarterly instalment} = \frac{\$5020}{12}$$
$$= \$418.33$$

iii **Purchase by Instalment**

This is a method which allows consumers to purchase goods by paying an initial deposit and then paying the balance in monthly or weekly instalments over a period of time.

In calculating the amount of each instalment the following steps can be followed:

Step 1: Calculate the initital deposit.
Deposit = Percentage rate × Cash price

Step 2: Calculate the balance owing (P).
P = Cash price – Deposit

Step 3: Calculate the interest to be paid on the balance owing (P).

$$I = \frac{P \times R \times N}{100}$$

Step 4: Calculate the total amount owed by the customer.
(ie P + I)

Step 5: Divide (P + I) by the number of instalments to find the value of each payment.

EXAMPLE

Spiro purchased a lounge suite (cash price $2800) by paying a 25% deposit and agreeing to pay the balance over 1½ years in monthly instalments. Interest of 10% is charged on the balance owing.

Calculate the amount of each payment.

SOLUTION

Step 1: Deposit = Percentage rate × Cash price

$= 25\% \times \$2800$

$= 0.25 \times \$2800$

$= \$700$

Step 2: P = Cash price – Deposit

$= \$2800 - \$700 = \$2100$

Step 3: $I = \dfrac{P \times R \times N}{100}$

$= \dfrac{2100 \times 10 \times 1.5}{100}$

$= \$315$

Step 4: Total amount owed = P + I

$= \$2100 + \$315$

$= \$2415$

Step 5: Monthly payment $= \dfrac{\$2415}{18}$

$= \$134.17$

A SIMPLIFYING ALGEBRAIC EXPRESSIONS

Below is a summary of the rules required in simplifying algebraic expressions.

Addition and Subtraction

- Can only add or subtract 'like' terms – ie those with the same pronumeral part.
- With **fractions** find the lowest common denominator (LCD), then add or subtract the numerators.

Multiplication

- Multiply out the numbers and pronumerals separately. Remember

$$+ \times + = +$$

$$+ \times - = -$$

$$- \times + = -$$

$$- \times - = +$$

- With **fractions**, multiply the numerators and denominators, then simplify.

Division

- Divide the numbers and pronumerals separately. Remember:

  $+ \div + = +$, $- \div + = -$,

  $+ \div - = -$, $- \div - = +$

- With **fractions**, change the division sign to a multiplication sign and multiply by the reciprocal of the fraction.

Removing Grouping Symbols

- Multiply the term outside the brackets by each term inside the brackets:

$$a(b + c) = a \times b + a \times c = ab + ac$$
$$a(b - c) = a \times b - a \times c = ab - ac$$

Factorisation

- To factorise an algebraic expression, find the HCF (Highest Common Factor) and place it outside the brackets.
- With **fractions**, the numerators and denominators should be factorised if possible and then simplified.

EXAMPLES I

Simplify the following:

i $2x + 4y - 5x - y$

ii $5x^2 - x - x^2 + 2x$

iii $3a \times 4a$

iv $16xy \div 8y$

v $\frac{2x}{3} - \frac{x}{5}$

vi $\frac{3y}{4} + \frac{5y}{7}$

vii $\frac{x}{9} \times \frac{6}{5x}$

viii $\frac{6x}{5} \div 12$

ix $3(2x + 5) - 3(4x - y) + 7(1 - 2y)$

x $\frac{4y}{7x} \times \frac{28x}{6}$

xi $\frac{3a}{14} \div \frac{9ab}{6}$

SOLUTIONS I

i $2x + 4y - 5x - y = 3y - 3x$

ii $5x^2 - x - x^2 + 2x = 4x^2 + x$

iii $3a \times 4a = 12a^2$ $(a \times a = a^2)$

iv $16xy \div 8y = \frac{16xy}{8y} = 2x$

v $\frac{2x}{3} - \frac{x}{5} = \frac{10x}{15} - \frac{3x}{15}$ (LCD = 15)

$= \frac{7x}{15}$

vi $\frac{3y}{4} + \frac{5y}{7} = \frac{21y}{28} + \frac{20y}{28}$ (LCD = 28)

$= \frac{41y}{28}$

vii $\frac{x}{9} \times \frac{6}{5x} = \frac{6x}{45x} = \frac{2}{15}$

viii $\frac{6x}{5} \div \frac{12}{1} = \frac{6x}{5} \times \frac{1}{12} = \frac{6x}{60} = \frac{x}{10}$

ix $3(2x + 5) - 3(4x - y) + 7(1 - 2y)$

$= 6x + 15 - 12x + 3y + 7 - 14y$

$= - 6x - 11y + 22$

x $\frac{4y}{7x} \times \frac{28x}{6} = \frac{112xy}{42x} = \frac{8y}{3}$

xi $\frac{3a}{14} \div \frac{9ab}{6} = \frac{3a}{14} \times \frac{6}{9ab} = \frac{18a}{126ab} = \frac{1}{7b}$

EXAMPLES 2

Factorise and simplify where possible:

i $2x - 4xy$ **ii** $81x^2 - 9xy$

iii $\frac{4x - 8}{2}$ **iv** $\frac{3x - 9y}{4x - 12y}$

SOLUTIONS I

i $2x - 4xy = 2x(1 - 2y)$ (HCF = $2x$)

ii $81x^2 - 9xy = 9x(9x - y)$ (HCF = $9x$)

iii $\frac{4x - 8}{2} = \frac{\cancel{4}^{2}(x - 2)}{\cancel{2}_{1}} = 2(x - 2)$

iv $\frac{3x - 9y}{4x - 12y} = \frac{3\cancel{(x - 3y)}}{4\cancel{(x - 3y)}} = \frac{3}{4}$

B INDICES

i Index Laws

1. $a^m \times a^n = a^{m+n}$	**2.** $(a^m)^n = a^{mn}$
3. $a^m \div a^n = a^{m-n}$	**4.** $(ab)^m = a^m b^m$
5. $a^0 = 1$	

EXAMPLES

Simplify:

i $x^5 \times x^3 + 2x^0$

ii $(2y^3)^3$

iii $(x^{\frac{1}{2}})^4$

iv $\frac{12x^3y^2}{15} \div \frac{9x^2y}{5}$

SOLUTIONS

i $x^5 \times x^3 + 2x^0 = x^5 \times x^3 \times 2$
$= 2x^{5+3} = 2x^8$

ii $(2y^3)^3 = 2^3(y^3)^3 = 8y^{3\times3} = 8y^9$

iii $(x^{\frac{1}{2}})^4 = x^{\frac{1}{2}\times4} = x^2$

iv $\frac{12x^3y^2}{15} \div \frac{9x^2y}{5} = \frac{12x^3y^2}{15} \times \frac{5}{9x^2y}$
$= \frac{60x^3y^2}{135x^2y}$
$= \frac{4xy}{9}$

ii Scientific Notation

Scientific notation is expressed as a number between 1 and 10 multiplied by a power of ten.

On the calculator scientific notation correct to n significant figures is given by:

[MODE] [8] [n]

EXAMPLES

Express the following in scientific notation correct to 2 significant figures:

i 1 000 000

ii 0.00657

iii 42 500

iv 953

SOLUTIONS

i $1\,000\,000 = 1.0 \times 10^6$ correct to 2 s.f.

ii $0.00657 = 6.57 \times 10^{-3}$

$= 6.6 \times 10^{-3}$ correct to 2 s.f.

iii $42\,500 = 4.25 \times 10^4$

$= 4.3 \times 10^4$ correct to 2 s.f.

iv $953 = 9.53 \times 10^2$

$= 9.5 \times 10^2$ correct to 2 s.f.

A SOLVING EQUATIONS

In solving equations, there is one golden rule:

> Whatever operation (+, –, ×, ÷) is done to one side of the equation must also be done to the other side.

The idea is to have the pronumerals end up on one side, and the numbers on the other.

EXAMPLES

Solve for x:

i $2x - 3(x + 5) = 10$

ii $\dfrac{x-1}{3} = \dfrac{1}{4}$

iii $\dfrac{x+1}{3} + \dfrac{2-x}{7} = 1$

iv $\dfrac{2x-1}{4} = \dfrac{x}{5}$

SOLUTIONS

i $2x - 3x - 15 = 10$ (expand brackets)

$-x = 25$ (mult. both sides by –1)

$\therefore x = -25$

ii $\frac{x-1}{3} = \frac{1}{4}$ (mult. both sides by 12)

$$12 \times \frac{x-1}{3} = 12 \times \frac{1}{4}$$

$$4(x-1) = 3 \quad \text{(cancelling terms)}$$

$$4x - 4 = 3$$

$$4x = 7$$

$$\therefore x = \frac{7}{4}$$

iii $\frac{x+1}{3} + \frac{2-x}{7} = 1$ (mult. both sides by 21)

$$21 \times \left(\frac{x+1}{3}\right) + 21 \times \left(\frac{2-x}{7}\right) = 1 \times 21$$

$$7(x+1) + 3(2-x) = 21 \quad \text{(cancelling terms)}$$

$$7x + 7 + 6 - 3x = 21$$

$$4x + 13 = 21$$

$$4x = 8$$

$$\therefore x = 2$$

iv $\frac{2x-1}{4} = \frac{x}{5}$

$$20 \times \left(\frac{2x-1}{4}\right) = 20 \times \left(\frac{x}{5}\right) \quad \text{(mult. both sides by 20)}$$

$$5(2x-1) = 4x \quad \text{(cancelling terms)}$$

$$10x - 5 = 4x$$

$$6x = 5$$

$$\therefore x = \frac{5}{6}$$

B SOLVING INEQUALITIES

In solving inequalities, you need to be aware of the following:

- Inequality sign is reversed if inequality is multiplied or divided by a negative number.
- Inequality sign is unchanged if inequality is multiplied or divided by a positive number.
- Inequality sign is unchanged if we add or subtract the same positive or negative number to both sides.

Solving inequalities gives a range of solutions when solved.

Graphing the Solution

To graph the solution of an inequality on a number line, there are two possible alternatives:

- ♦ A solid dot ● plus a line and arrow pointing right for $\geqslant$ and arrow pointing left for $\leqslant$.
- ♦ An open circle ○ plus a line and arrow pointing right for > and arrow pointing left for <.

EXAMPLES

Solve the following inequalities, then graph the solution on a number line.

i $3 + 2x \geqslant 5$ **ii** $x - (2x + 1) > 4$

SOLUTIONS

i $3 + 2x \geqslant 5$

$2x \geqslant 2$

Subtracting 3 from both sides doesn't change the sign.

$\frac{2x}{2} \geqslant \frac{2}{2}$

$\therefore x \geqslant 1$

Dividing both sides by 2 doesn't change the sign.

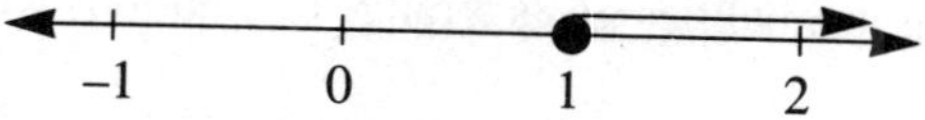

Note: • Solid dot ● as ⩾ sign.

• Arrow points right as ⩾ sign.

SOLUTIONS

ii $x - (2x + 1) > 4$

$x - 2x - 1 > 4$

$-x - 1 > 4$

$-x > 5$

Adding 1 to both sides doesn't change the sign

$-1 \times -x < -1 \times 5$

$\therefore x < -5$

Multiplying both sides by – 1 changes the sign.

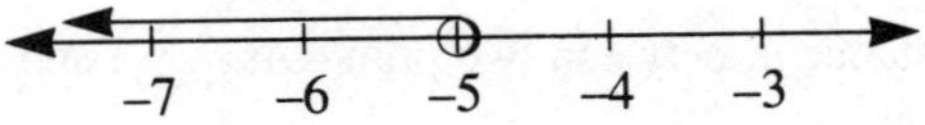

Note: • Open circle ○ as < sign (no =).

• Arrow points left as < sign.

CHAPTER 6:
THE NUMBER PLANE AND GRAPHS OF LINES & CURVES

Although students may learn from first principles how to calculate the distance between two points, the midpoint of an interval and the gradient of a line, it is far more efficient to simply apply the formulae shown below.

In addition, these formulae form part of the HSC course, and are the recommended method for solving these problems.

A THE DISTANCE FORMULA

The distance d, between two points $A(x_1, y_1)$ and $B(x_2, y_2)$:

$$d = \sqrt{(x_2 - x_1)^2 + (y_2 - y_1)^2}$$

B THE MIDPOINT FORMULA

The midpoint M, of the interval joining $A(x_1, y_1)$ and $B(x_2, y_2)$:

$$M\ (x,\ y) = \left(\frac{x_1 + x_2}{2}, \frac{y_1 + y_2}{2}\right)$$

C THE GRADIENT FORMULA

The gradient m, of a line joining 2 points $A(x_1, y_1)$ and $B(x_2, y_2)$:

$$m = \frac{y_2 - y_1}{x_2 - x_1}$$

EXAMPLE

For the points $A(1, 2)$ and $B(5, -1)$, find:

i The distance AB.

ii The midpoint of AB.

iii The gradient of the interval AB.

SOLUTION

For the points $A(1, 2)$ and $B(5, -1)$, find:

i $d = \sqrt{(x_2 - x_1)^2 + (y_2 - y_1)^2}$
$= \sqrt{(5 - 1)^2 + (-1 - 2)^2}$
$= \sqrt{4^2 + (-3)^2}$
$= \sqrt{16 + 9}$
$= \sqrt{25} = 5$ units

$(x_1, y_1) = (1, 2)$
$(x_2, y_2) = (5, -1)$

$(-3)^2 = -3 \times -3 = 9$

ii $M(x, y) = \left(\frac{x_1 + x_2}{2}, \frac{y_1 + y_2}{2}\right)$

$= \left(\frac{1 + 5}{2}, \frac{2 + (-1)}{2}\right)$

$= \left(\frac{6}{2}, \frac{1}{2}\right) = \left(3, \frac{1}{2}\right)$

iii $m = \frac{y_2 - y_1}{x_2 - x_1} = \frac{-1 - 2}{5 - 1} = -\frac{3}{4}$

D GRAPHS OF STRAIGHT LINES

i Graphing a Line

To graph a straight line, follow these steps:

Step 1 Set up a table of values at $x = 0, 1, 2$ and find their equivalent y-values.

Step 2 Plot the points on a number plane.

Step 3 Join the points by a straight line. Place arrows on the ends and label the graph.

For an example refer to page 33.

ii Horizontal and Vertical Lines

- **Horizontal lines** are parallel to the x-axis and are in the form $y = b$.
- **Vertical lines** are parallel to the y-axis and are in the form $x = a$.

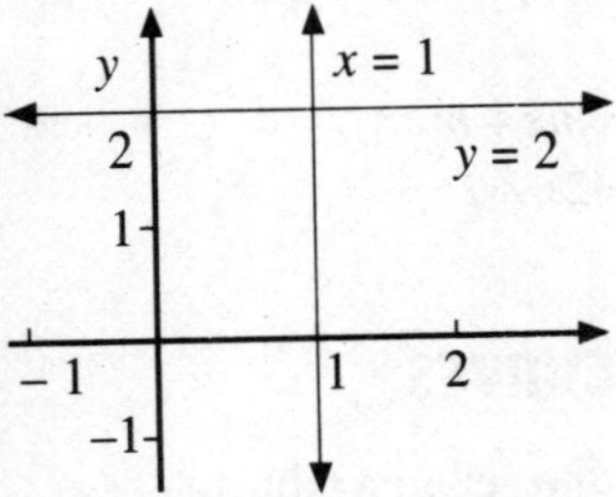

The diagram shows the lines $y = 2$, parallel to the x-axis and $x = 1$, parallel to the y-axis

iii The Equation $y = mx + b$

For a straight line written in the form $y = mx + b$, m is the gradient of the line and b is the y-intercept.

This form of the straight-line equation can be used to write the equation of a line, given the gradient and y-intercept.

EXAMPLE

A line passes through the points $A(0, 2)$ and $(-1, 0)$. Sketch the line on a number plane, hence find its equation.

SOLUTIONS

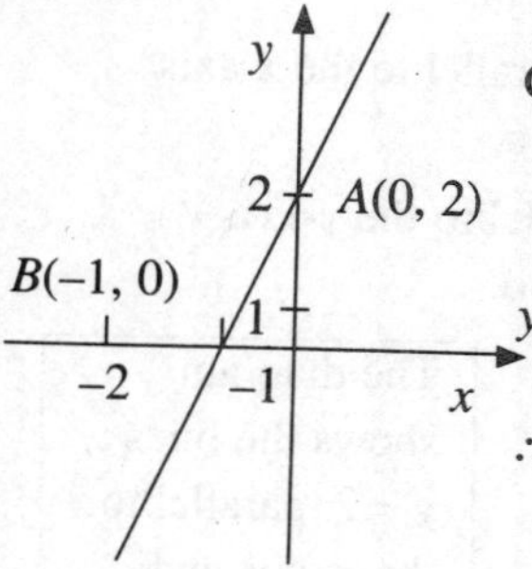

Gradient: $m = \dfrac{y_2 - y_1}{x_2 - x_1}$

$= \dfrac{2 - 0}{0 - -1} = \dfrac{2}{1} = 2$

y-intercept: $b = 2$

$\therefore y = mx + b$

$= 2x + 2$

E GRAPHS OF OTHER CURVES

To graph curves, students need to set up a table of values and then join the dots to form the curve.

Students need to be familiar with the following 3 basic curves and any slight variations on them.

Refer to page 34 for an illustrated example of how to sketch a curve with a slight variation on the basic curve.

THE NUMBER PLANE AND GRAPHS OF LINES & CURVES

1 The Parabola $y = x^2$

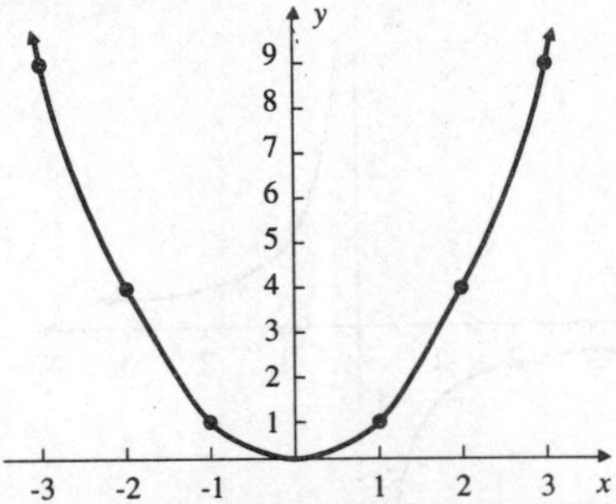

x	-3	-2	-1	0	1	2	3
y	9	4	1	0	1	4	9

2 The Cubic Equation $y = x^3$

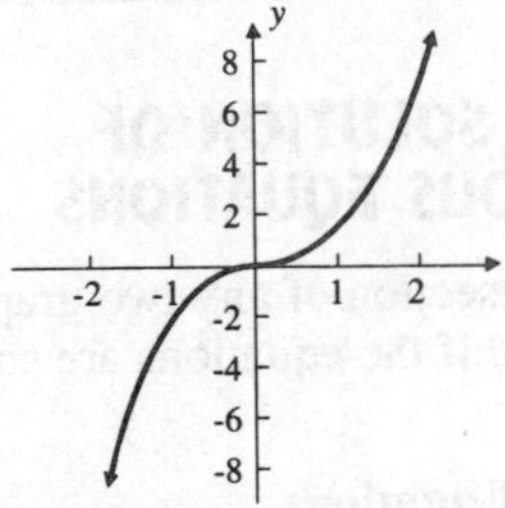

x	-2	-1	0	1	2
y	-8	-1	0	1	8

3 The Hyperbola $y = \frac{1}{x}$

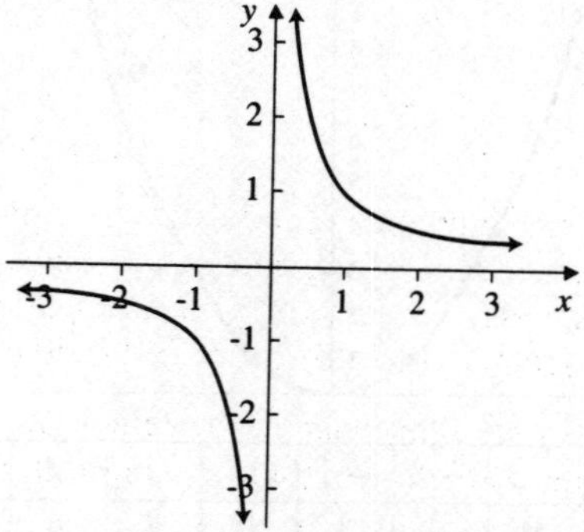

x	-2	-1	-0.5	0.5	1	2
y	-0.5	-1	-2	2	1	0.5

F GRAPHICAL SOLUTION OF SIMULTANEOUS EQUATIONS

The points of intersection of any two graphs represent the solutions found if the equations are solved simultaneously.

i Two Linear Equations

Two straight lines can intersect (if at all) at only one point, ie there is only **one** common solution.

EXAMPLE

Find by graphical means the common solution to the lines:

$y = 2 - x$ and $y = 5 - 2x$

SOLUTION

$y = 2 - x$

x	0	1	2
y	2	-1	0

$y = 5 - 2x$

x	0	1	2
y	5	3	1

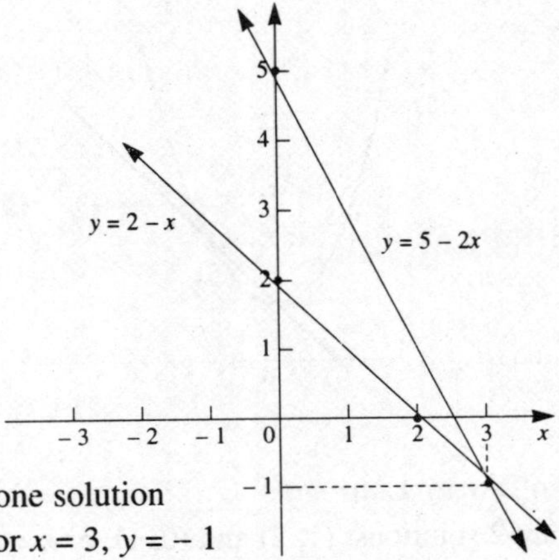

There is one solution
(3, – 1), or $x = 3$, $y = -1$

ii Using Other Graphs

EXAMPLE

Find the solutions to the curves:

$y = x^2 + 1$ and $y = x + 1$

$y = x^2 + 1$

x	– 2	– 1	0	1	2
y	5	2	1	2	5

$y = x + 1$

x	– 1	0	1
y	0	1	2

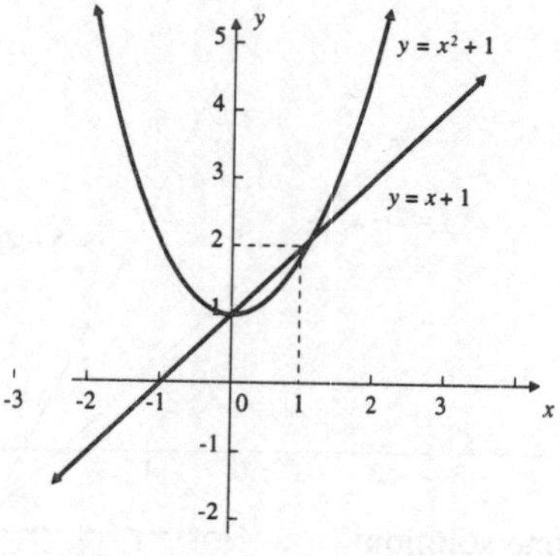

There are 2 solutions: (1, 2) and (0, 1), or $x = 1$, $y = 2$ and $x = 0$, $y = 1$

A BASIC STATISTICAL FORMULAE

- Range = highest score – lowest score
- Mode = most common score
- Mean = $\dfrac{\text{total of all scores}}{\text{number of scores}} = \dfrac{\Sigma x}{n} = \dfrac{\Sigma xf}{\Sigma f}$
- Median = middle score, when scores are arranged in ascending order.

Note: If scores are even, then the median is the average of the two middle scores.

B STATISTICAL NOTATION

x = score

f = frequency

cf = cumulative frequency

$\bar{x}$ = mean

Σ = sum

Σf = sum of frequency column

xf = (score) × (frequency)

Σxf = sum of xf column

C SIMPLE DISTRIBUTIONS

In this course students need to be able to set up a frequency distribution table and from that graph the:

- **i** histogram and its associated frequency polygon.
- **ii** cumulative frequency histogram and its associated cumulative frequency polygon.

EXAMPLE

Twenty students were each given a coin and asked to toss it four times. Each student then recorded the number of heads attained. The results were as follows:

2	3	1	2	2	2	4	2	3	1
3	1	2	3	1	0	1	2	4	2

i Construct a frequency distribution table.

ii Construct:

- **a** A frequency histogram and its associated frequency polygon.
- **b** A cumulative frequency histogram and its associated cumulative frequency polygon.

SOLUTION

i

Score (x)	Tally	Frequency (f)	Cumulative Frequency (cf)	xf
0	I	1	1	0
1	~~IIII~~	5	6	5
2	~~IIII~~ III	8	14	16
3	IIII	4	18	12
4	II	2	20	8

ii a

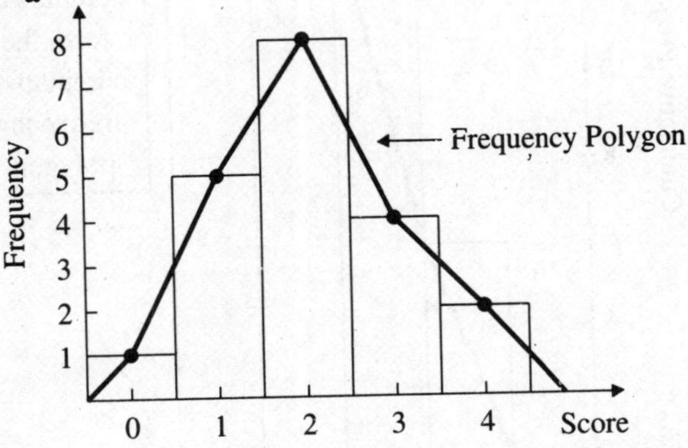

Note: We join the midpoints of the columns to form the frequency polygon.

b

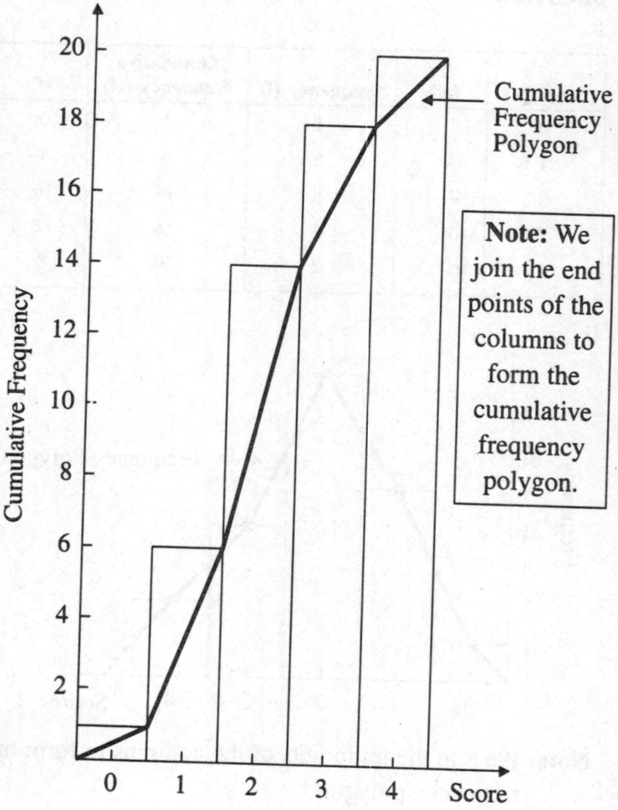
Cumulative Frequency
20
18
16
14
12
10
8
6
4
2
0
1
2
3
4
Score
Cumulative Frequency Polygon
Note: We join the end points of the columns to form the cumulative frequency polygon.

D DOT PLOTS

A dot plot is another way of displaying information. A dot is placed for each score read off the data.

E STEM AND LEAF PLOTS

This is yet another way of displaying data.

The **stem** represents the first digit or digits of a number and the **leaf** represents the final digit. For example:

	Stem	Leaf
32	3	2
700	70	0

After the initial plot, the digits in the leaf column should be arranged in increasing order to allow a quicker and clearer way of reading the results.

F RELATIVE FREQUENCY

Relative frequency is a measure of how often a particular score may arise:

$$\text{Relative frequency of a score} = \frac{\text{frequency of score}}{\text{total frequency}} = \frac{f}{\Sigma f}$$

G STANDARD DEVIATION AND THE NORMAL DISTRIBUTION

i Standard Deviation

Standard deviation is a common measure of how spread the data is, relative to the mean.

A large standard deviation means the scores are widely spread, while a small standard deviation means that the scores are closer to the mean.

The standard deviation is determined using a calculator (refer to next section for details).

The symbol σn means standard deviation.

ii The Normal Distribution

In a normal distribution:

- 68% of all scores are within 1 standard deviation from the mean.
- 95% of all scores are within 2 standard deviations from the mean.
- 99.7% of all scores are within 3 standard deviations from the mean.

The Normal Curve

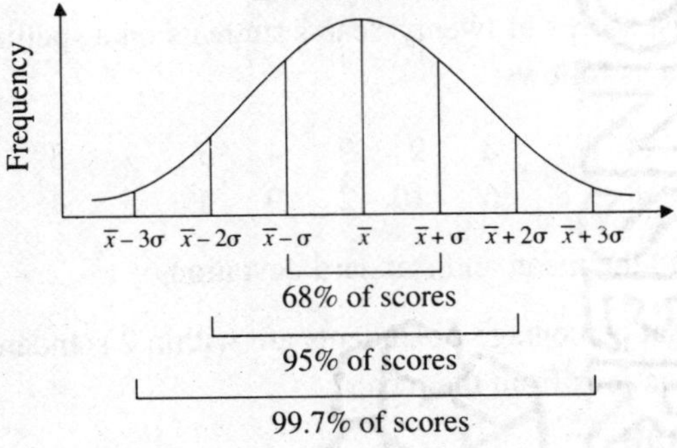

H STATISTICAL MODE ON THE CALCULATOR

The calculator, once switched into SD mode, can be used to work out the mean and standard deviation automatically.

Step 1: [MODE] [•] (puts calculator in SD mode)

Step 2: Enter each score individually followed by the [M+] key:
score [M+] score [M+] etc.

Step 3: [INV] [7] gives mean ($\bar{x}$)
[INV] [8] gives SD (σn)

EXAMPLE

The test scores of twenty Year 1 students on a spelling test are as follows:

5	4	7	8	9	9	4	7	7	8
7	8	8	6	10	2	9	1	5	4

i Find the mean and standard deviation.

ii What percentage of students are within 2 standard deviations from the mean?

SOLUTION

i On the calculator: [MODE] [•]
5 [M+] 4 [M+] 7 [M+] etc.
[INV] [7] : $\bar{x}$ = mean = 6.4
[INV] [8] : σn = SD = 2.4 to 1 d.p.

ii Now $\bar{x} + 2\sigma n = 6.4 + 2 \times 2.4 = 11.2$
and $\bar{x} - 2\sigma n = 6.4 - 2 \times 2.4 = 1.6$

There is only one score outside these ranges (namely 1), ie 19 are within.

∴ percentage of students that are within 2 SD

$$= \frac{19}{20} \times \frac{100}{1} = 95\%$$

I PROBABILITY

The probability of an event can be defined as the likelihood of an event occurring.

Thus, in a trial with n equally likely outcomes, the probability that a particular event E occurs is given by:

$$P(E) = \frac{\text{the number of ways } E \text{ can occur}}{\text{the total possible outcomes } (n)}$$

Note:
- All probabilities must lie between 0 and 1 (ie $0 \leqslant P(E) \leqslant 1$)
- If an event E is **certain**, then $P(E) = 1$
- If an event E is **impossible**, then $P(E) = 0$

Probability the Event Does Not Occur

Since the probabilities of all possible outcomes must add up to 1 then:

> P(the event E doesn't occur)
> = 1 – P(event E does occur)
> ie $P(\bar{E}) = 1 - P(E)$
>
> **Note:** $P(\bar{E})$ and $P(E)$ are called complementary events.

EXAMPLE

A box contains 4 red, 6 white, 9 green and 2 black balls. If one ball is chosen, find the probability it is not green.

SOLUTION

$P(\bar{E}) = 1 - P(E)$

P(the ball is not green) = 1 – P (the ball is green)

$$= 1 - \frac{\text{No. of green balls}}{\text{Total no. of balls}}$$

$$= 1 - \frac{9}{21}$$

$$= \frac{12}{21} = \frac{4}{7}$$

There are a number of different types of graphs that students need to know.

A COLUMN GRAPHS

Column graphs use vertical columns with spaces in between them to represent data.

EXAMPLE

A survey was conducted to find the number of matches in each of 12 boxes. The results are shown on the column graph below:

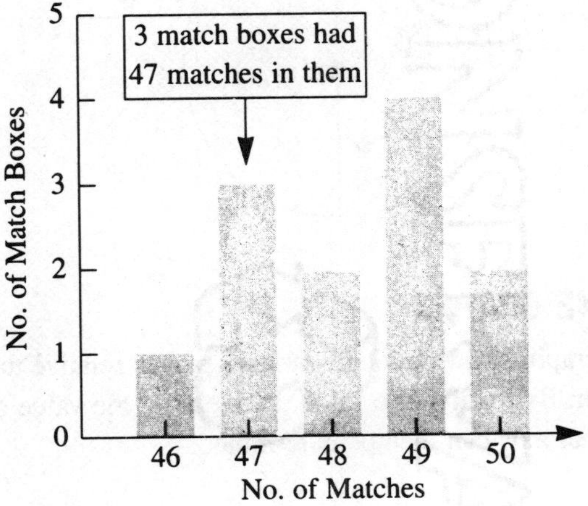

B SECTOR GRAPHS (Pie Charts)

Pie charts use a circle cut up into different size sectors to represent data.

EXAMPLE

The pie chart below shows the means of transport used by students to get to school.

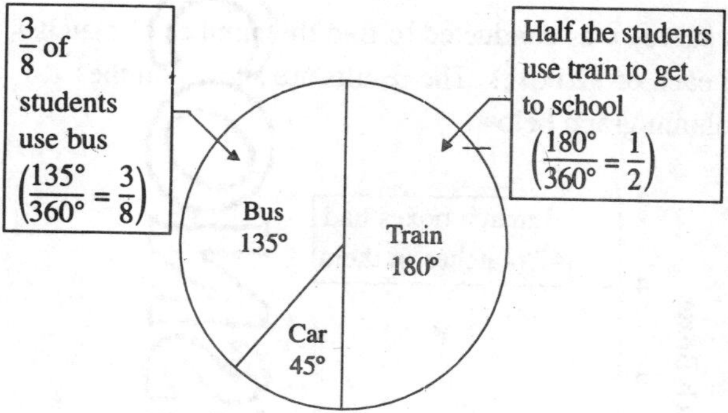

C LINE GRAPHS

Line graphs show how one variable moves relative to another. By reading the value on one axis, the value on the other axis can then be determined.

EXAMPLE

The rainfall in a particular town is graphed over a period of a year.

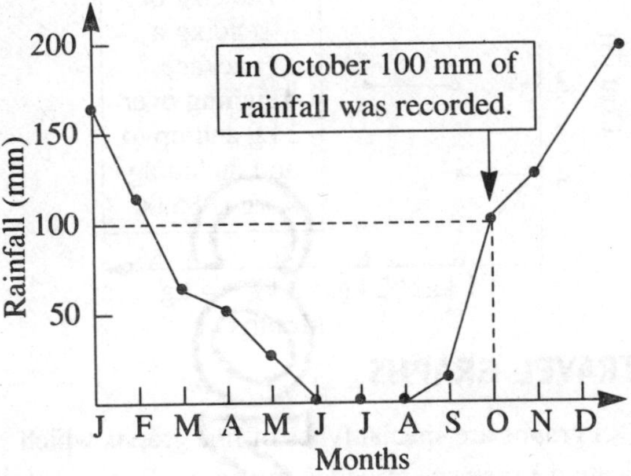

D STEP GRAPHS

Step graphs use a series of horizontal lines with definitive breaks between them to represent data.

EXAMPLE

The cost of posting a package is shown in the following step graph:

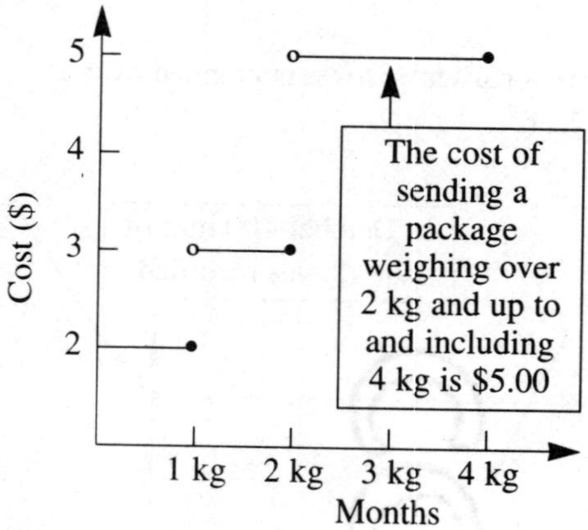

E TRAVEL GRAPHS

Travel graphs are special types of line graphs which indicate the distance travelled over time. Some useful characteristics are:

- Average speed = $\dfrac{\text{Distance}}{\text{Time}}$
- The **steeper** the line the **faster** the speed.
- A **flat** line means stationary.

EXAMPLE

The journey of a car from town A to town B is shown below:

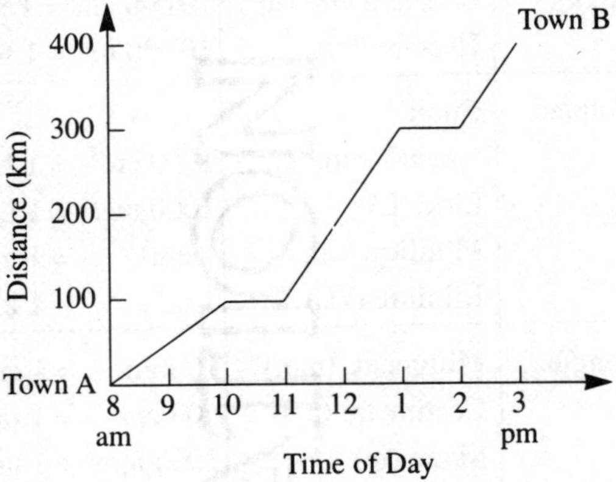

i When and for how long did the car stop?

ii What was the average speed for the whole trip?

SOLUTION

i At 10 am for 1 hour, and at 1 pm for 1 hour.

ii $\text{Speed} = \dfrac{\text{Distance}}{\text{Time}} = \dfrac{400}{7} = 57.1 \text{ km/h}$

A TABLE OF IMPORTANT MEASUREMENTS

Quantity	Unit	Conversions
Area	Square metre (m^2) Hectare (ha)	10 000 cm^2 = 1 m^2 10 000 m^2 = 1 ha
Volume	Cubic centimetre (cm^3) Litre (L) Millilitre (mL) Kilolitre (kL)	1000 cm^3 = 1 L 1000 mL = 1 L 1 cm^3 = 1 mL 1 m^3 = 1 kL
Length	Millimetre (mm) Centimetre (cm) Metre (m) Kilometre (km)	10 mm = 1 cm 100 cm = 1 m 1000 mm = 1 m 1000 m = 1 km
Mass	Gram (g) Kilogram (kg) Tonne (t)	1000 mg = 1 g 1000 g = 1 kg 1000 kg = 1 t
Capacity	Millilitre (mL) Litre (L) Megalitre (ML)	1000 mL = 1 L 1000 L = 1 kL 1000 kL = 1 ML

ii Less Common Units of Measurement

Prefix	Symbol	Meaning
giga	G	1 000 000 000
meg	M	1 000 000
kilo	k	1000
milli	m	$\frac{1}{1000}$
micro	μ	$\frac{1}{1\,000\,000}$
nano	n	$\frac{1}{1\,000\,000\,000}$

B PERIMETER

Name	Shape	Perimeter
Square	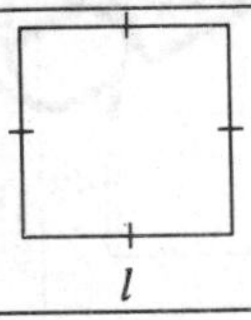	$4l$

B PERIMETER

Name	Shape	Perimeter
Rectangle	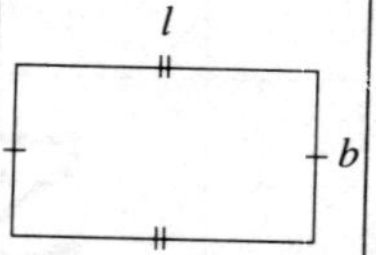	$2l + 2b$
Circle	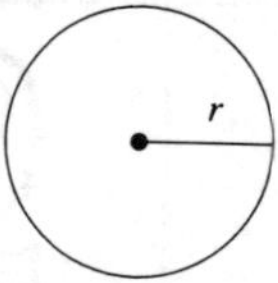	$2\pi r$ (or πd)

C AREA

Name	Shape	Area
Square	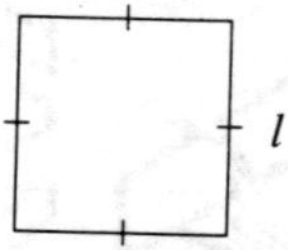	l^2 (length squared)
Rectangle	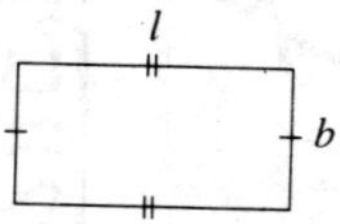	lb (length $\times$ breadth)

Name	Shape	Area
Triangle	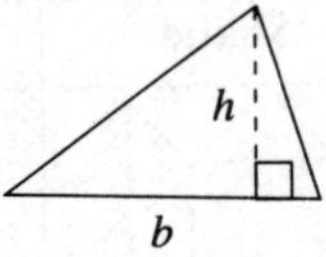	$\frac{1}{2}bh$ ($\frac{1}{2}$ base × height)
Parallelogram	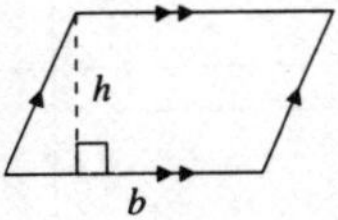	bh (base × height)
Rhombus	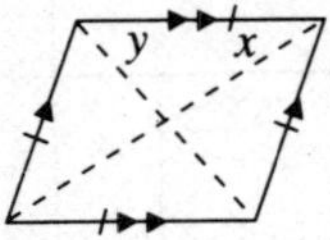	$\frac{1}{2}xy$ ($\frac{1}{2}$ product of diagonals)
Trapezium	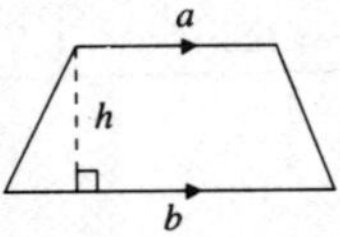	$\frac{1}{2}h\,(a + b)$ ($\frac{1}{2}$ sum of parallel sides × height)
Circle		πr^2 (pi × radius squared)

D SURFACE AREA

Name	Shape	Area
Cube	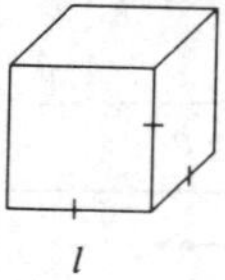	$6l^2$
Rectangular Prism	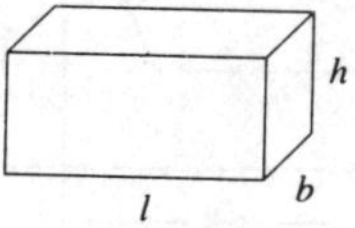	$2(lb + lh + bh)$
Cylinder	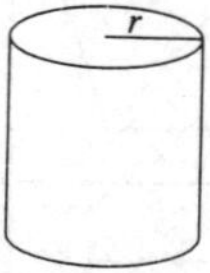	$2\pi rh$ (open) $2\pi rh + 2\pi r^2$ (closed)

E VOLUME

Name	Shape	Volume
Cube	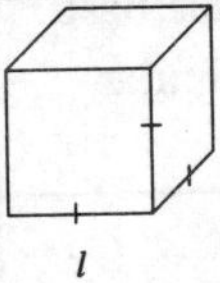	l^3
Rectangular Prism	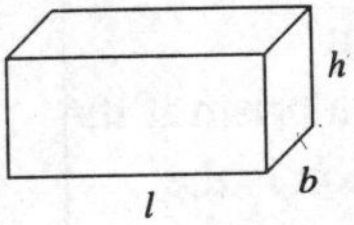	lbh
Cone	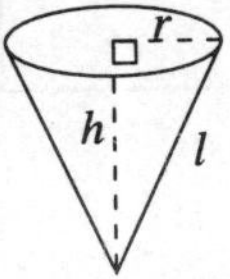	$\frac{1}{3}\pi r^2 h$
Sphere	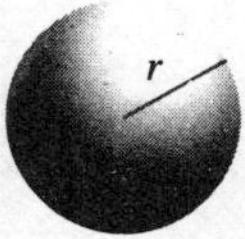	$\frac{4}{3}\pi r^3$

Shape	Volume
Any Pyramid Where A = area of the base h = perpendicular height	$\frac{1}{3}Ah$
Any Prism Where A = area of the base h = height **Note:** A solid is a prism if its cross-section is the same throughout the shape.	Ah

A PYTHAGORAS' THEOREM

Pythagoras' theorem states that in any right-angled triangle:

> 'the square of the hypotenuse is equal to the sum of the squares on the other two sides'.

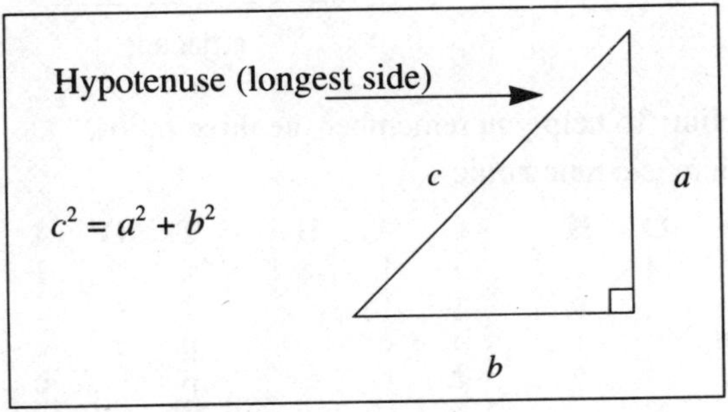

$$c^2 = a^2 + b^2$$

B TRIGONOMETRIC RATIOS

These ratios are vitally important and should be memorised.

They are based on any right-angled triangle.

$$\sin\theta = \frac{\text{opposite}}{\text{hypotenuse}} \quad \text{(SOH)}$$

$$\cos\theta = \frac{\text{adjacent}}{\text{hypotenuse}} \quad \text{(CAH)}$$

$$\tan\theta = \frac{\text{opposite}}{\text{adjacent}} \quad \text{(TOA)}$$

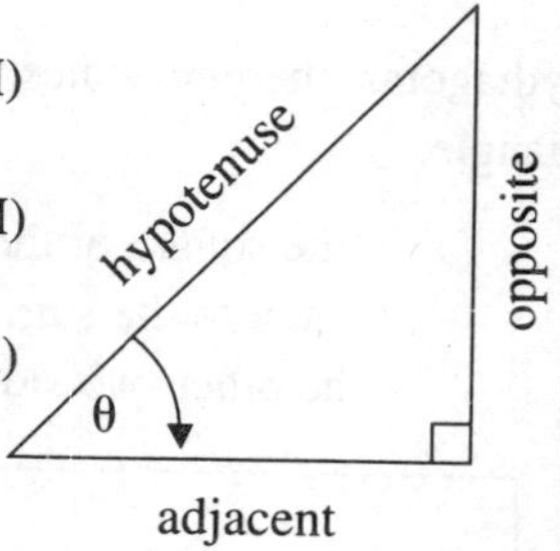

Hint: To help you remember the three ratios, here is a mnemonic:

S	**O**	**H**	**C**	**A**	**H**	**T**	**O**	**A**
Shame	On	Henry	Crying	After	He	Tripped	Over	Alice

i Degrees and Minutes

A degree may be subdivided into 60 equal parts called minutes.

$1^{\circ} = 60'$ (minutes) $\quad 1' = 60''$ (seconds)

Students need to know how to use their calculator when it comes to angles expressed in degrees and minutes.

FOR EXAMPLE

- $\cos 32°24' = 0.8412$ (to 4 d.p.)

Calculator: 32 [°'''] 24 [°'''] [COS]

- $\sin\theta = 0.475$
  $\therefore\ \theta = 28°22'$ (to the nearest minute)

ii Finding Sides and Angles

Trigonometric ratios can be used to find the length of a side, given an acute angle and one side, or the size of an angle given two sides in a right-angled triangle.

EXAMPLE 1

Find the length of *AB* and *BC* correct to 1 decimal place.

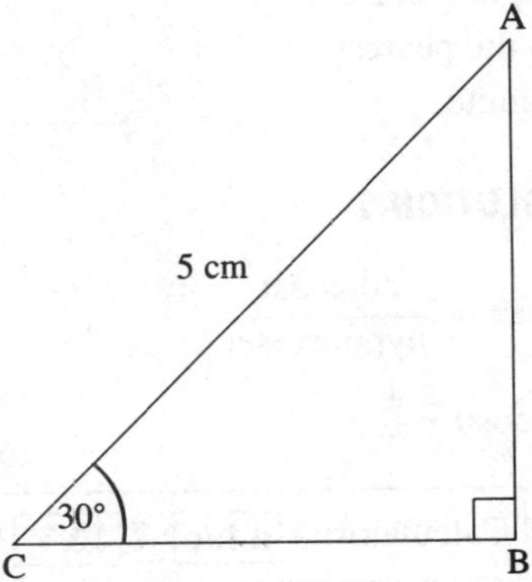

SOLUTION 1

$$\sin\theta = \frac{\text{opposite}}{\text{hypotenuse}}$$

$$\therefore \sin 30^\circ = \frac{AB}{5}$$

$$AB = 5 \times \sin 30^\circ$$
$$= 2.5 \text{ cm}$$

$$\cos\theta = \frac{\text{adjacent}}{\text{hypotenuse}}$$

$$\therefore \cos\theta = \frac{BC}{5}$$

$$BC = 5 \times \cos 30^\circ$$
$$= 4.3 \text{ cm}$$

EXAMPLE 2

Find the size of angle θ correct to the nearest minute.

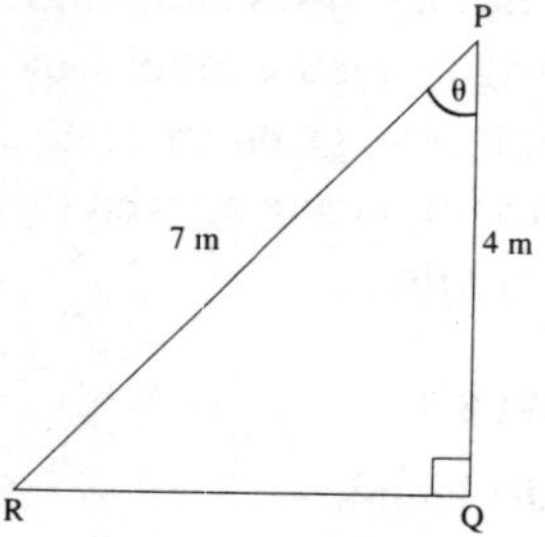

SOLUTION 2

$$\cos\theta = \frac{\text{adjacent}}{\text{hypotenuse}}$$

$$\therefore \cos\theta = \frac{4}{7}$$

ie $\theta = 55^\circ 9'$
to the nearest min.

Calculator: 4 [a b/c] 7 [INV] [COS] [INV] [o’’’]

C ANGLES OF ELEVATION AND DEPRESSION

Angles of elevation and depression are always measured **from the horizontal.**

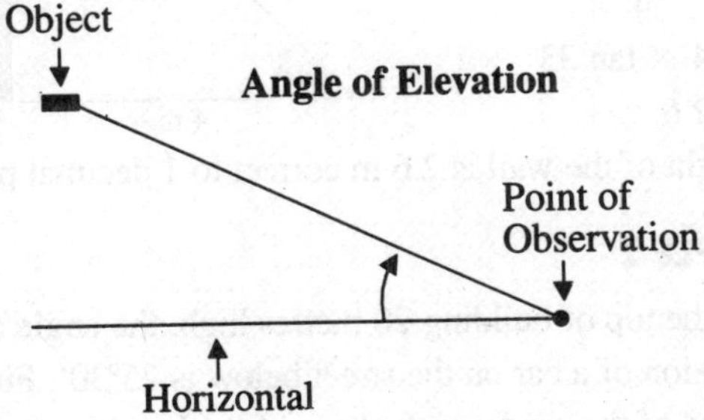

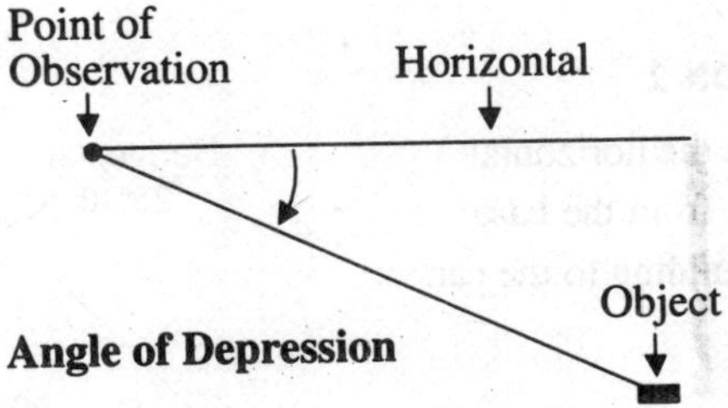

EXAMPLE 1

Find the height of wall which has an angle of elevation of 33° at a point 4 metres from its base.

SOLUTION 1

Let the height of the wall be x m.

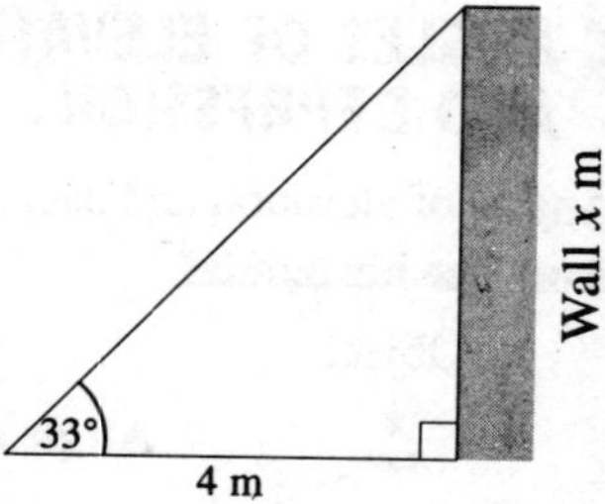

$$\tan 33° = \frac{x}{4}$$

$$\therefore x = 4 \times \tan 33°$$
$$\approx 2.6$$

$\therefore$ Height of the wall is 2.6 m correct to 1 decimal place.

EXAMPLE 2

From the top of building 20 metres high, the angle of depression of a car on the street below is 25°30′. Find the distance of the car from the base of the building (to the nearest metre).

SOLUTION 2

Let x be the horizontal distance from the base of the building to the car.

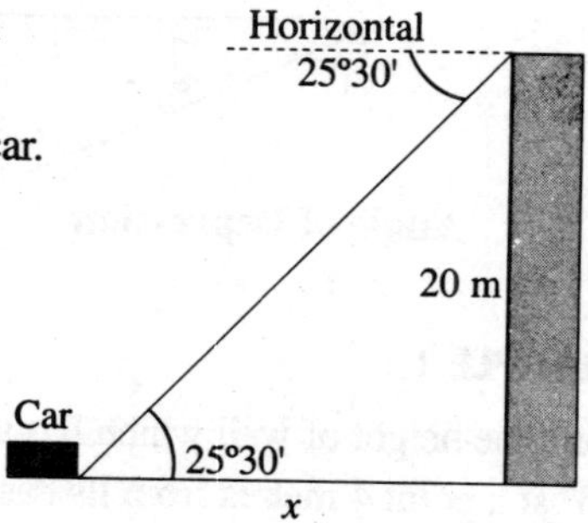

$$\tan 25°30' = \frac{20}{x}$$

$$\therefore x = \frac{20}{\tan 25°30'}$$

$$= 41.93087198$$

$$= 42 \text{ m to the nearest metre}$$

$\therefore$ The car is 42 m away from the base of the building.

D BEARINGS

Bearings are always measured **clockwise** from **north.** They are expressed in the form:

XXX°T where 000 ≤ XXX ≤ 360

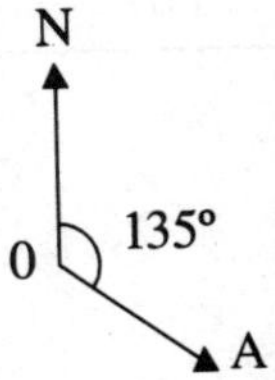

Bearing of
A from 0
is 135°T

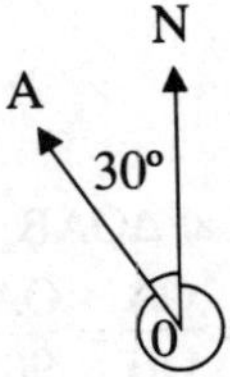

Bearing of
A from 0
is 330°T

EXAMPLE 1

A ship sails 90 km at a bearing of 150° from a lighthouse. How far east is the ship from the lighthouse?

SOLUTION 1

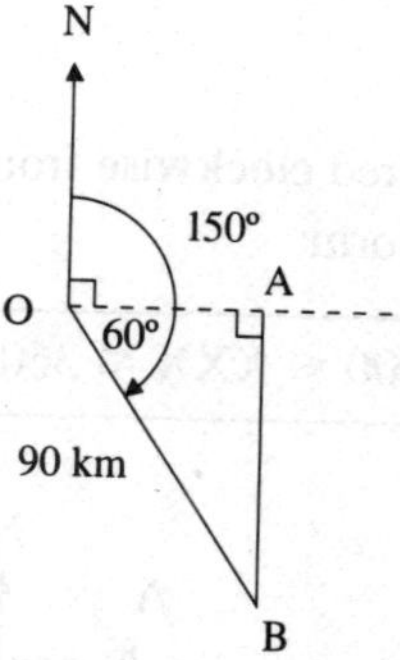

$\angle AOB$
$= 150° - 90°$
$= 60°$

Looking at ΔOAB

$$\cos 60° = \frac{OA}{OB} = \frac{OA}{90}$$

$$\therefore OA = 90 \times \cos 60°$$
$$= 45 \text{ km}$$

EXAMPLE 2

A ship sails due west from O for 40 km and then decides to sail 25 km due south. Find the bearing of the ship from O to the nearest degree.

SOLUTION 2

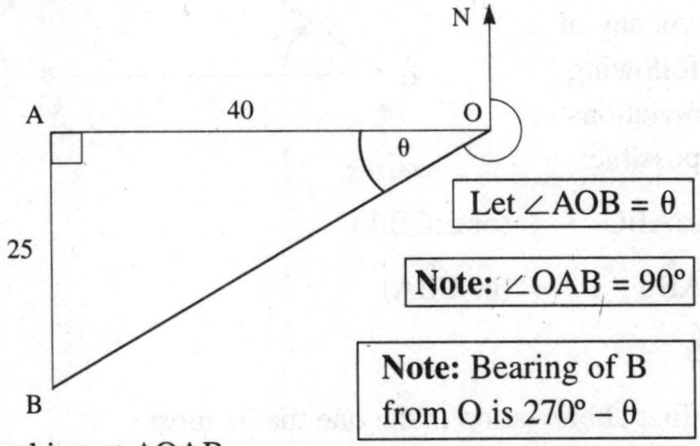

Looking at ΔOAB:

$$\tan\theta = \frac{AB}{OA} = \frac{25}{40} = 0.625$$

$\therefore \theta = 32^\circ$ to the nearest degree

Now bearing of B from O $= 270^\circ - \theta$

$$= 270^\circ - 32^\circ$$

$$= 238^\circ$$

$\therefore$ Bearing of the ship from O is 238°T.

A NAMING ANGLES

In naming angles, the vertex must be the middle letter.

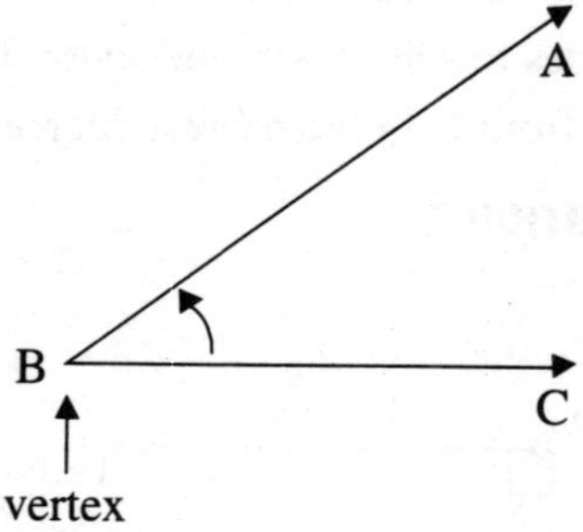

To name the angle shown, any of the following abbreviations are possible:

- $\angle ABC$ (or $\angle CBA$)
- $A\hat{B}C$ (or $C\hat{B}A$)
- $\hat{B}$

The first abbreviation is the one that is most commonly used.

B TYPES OF ANGLES

Students need to be familiar with the following types of angles:

Angle	Diagram	Details
Acute Angle	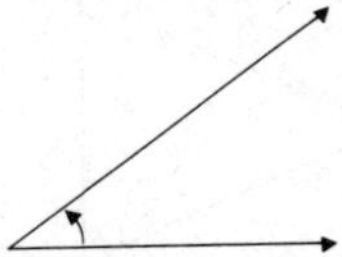	angle less than 90°
Obtuse Angle	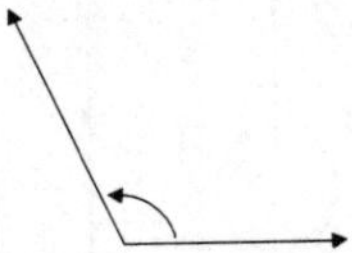	angle between 90° and 180°
Right Angle	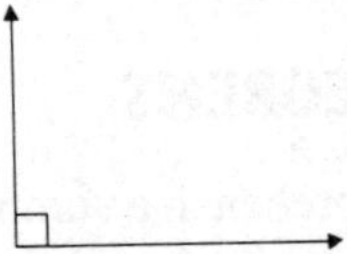	angle exactly 90°
Straight Angle		measures exactly 180°

Angle	Diagram	Details
Reflex Angle	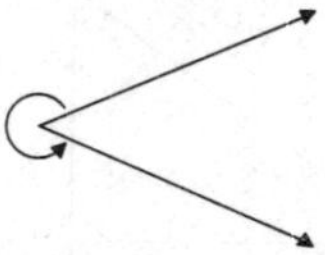	angle between 180° and 360°
Revolution	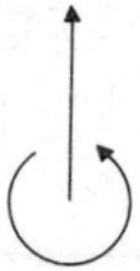	angle exactly 360°

C GEOMETRY THEOREMS

Listed below is a comprehensive summary of all the geometric theorems and rules required in this course.

Students with a sound understanding of these theorems should perform at a very high level in any geometry exam questions.

1	**Complementary** angles sum to 90°	
2	**Supplementary** angles sum to 180°	
3	Angles in a straight line sum to 180°	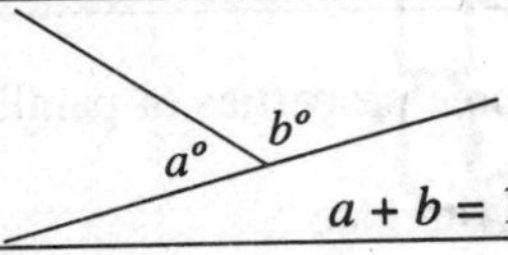 $a + b = 180°$
4	Angles which meet at a point sum to 360°	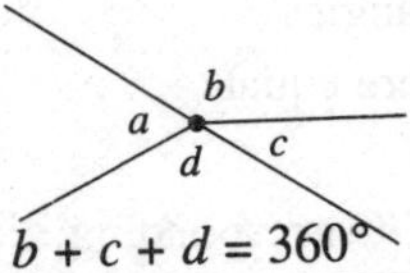 $a + b + c + d = 360°$
5	Vertically opposite angles are equal	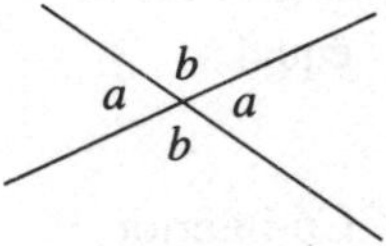
6	Angle sum of a triangle = 180° $a + b + c = 180°$	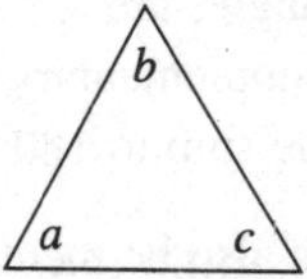
7	Angle sum of a quadrilateral = 360° $a + b + c + d = 360°$	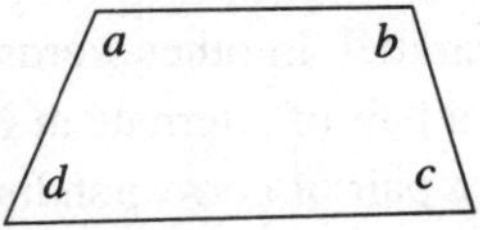

8 Angle sum of any polygon = $(2n - 4) \times 90°$
where n = number of sides

9 Three properties of parallel lines:

i Alternate angles are equal

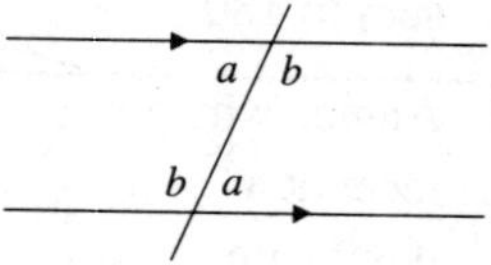

ii Corresponding angles are equal

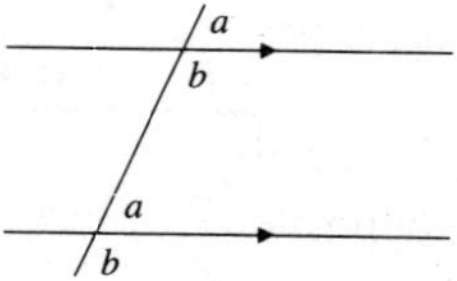

iii Co-interior angles are supplementary (ie sum to 180°)

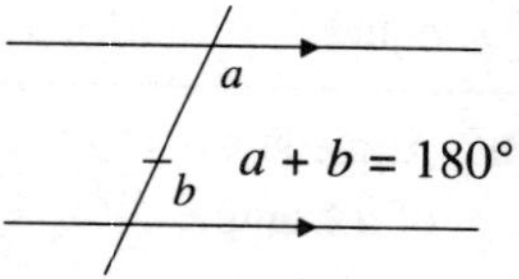

It should also be mentioned that these properties may be used to check whether two lines are parallel. In other words, two lines are parallel if:

- a pair of alternate angles are equal; or
- a pair of corresponding angles are equal; or
- a pair of co-interior angles are supplementary.

10 If two sides of a triangle are equal then the triangle is **isosceles**. Base angles of isosceles triangles are equal.

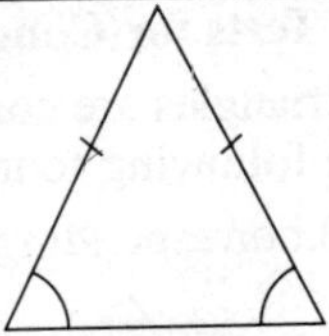

11 If three sides of a triangle are equal then the triangle is **equilateral**. All angles of equaliteral triangles are equal to 60°.

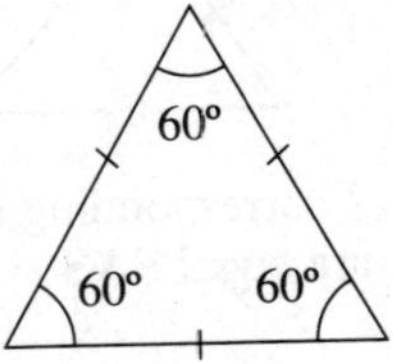

12 Congruent Triangles

Two triangles are congruent if they have exactly the same **shape** and **size** (ie the 3 sides and angles of one triangle equal the 3 sides and angles of the other triangle).

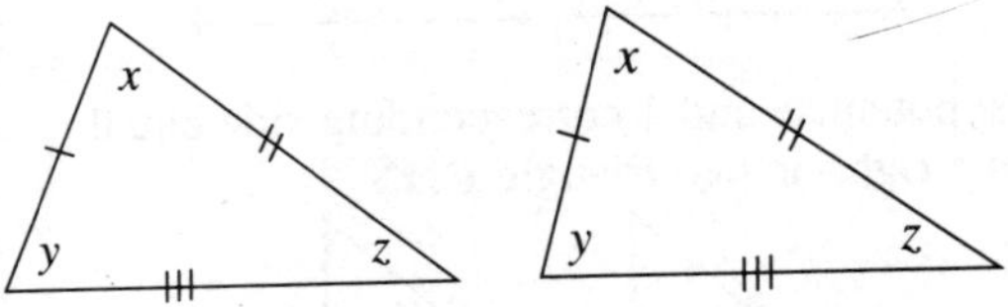

The symbol ≡ means 'is congruent to'.

Four Tests for Congruent Triangles

Two triangles are congruent if they satisfy any of the following four tests:

1 3 corresponding sides are equal **SSS**

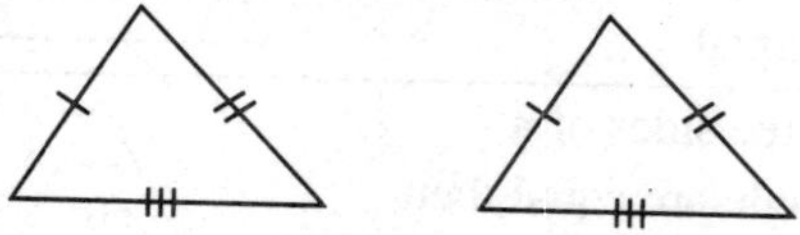

2 2 corresponding sides and the included angle are equal **SAS**

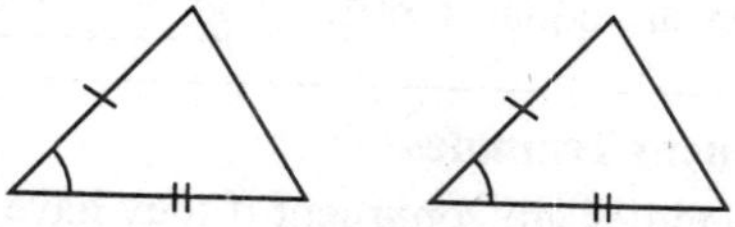

3 2 corresponding angles and 1 corresponding side are equal **AAS**

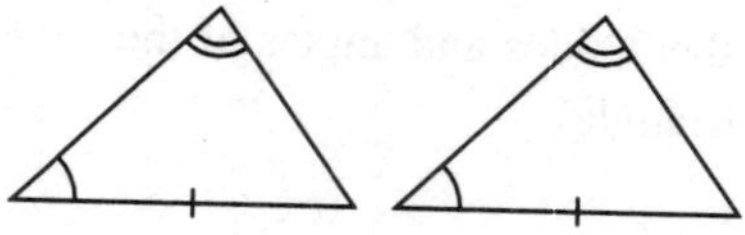

4 Hypotenuse and 1 corresponding side equal in a right-angled triangle **RHS**

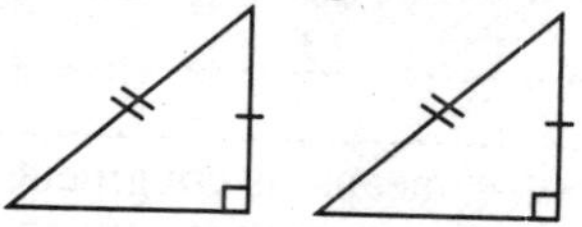

13 Similar Triangles

Two triangles are similar (ie same **shape** but not **size**) if they satisfy any of the following three tests:

1 All corresponding angles are equal.

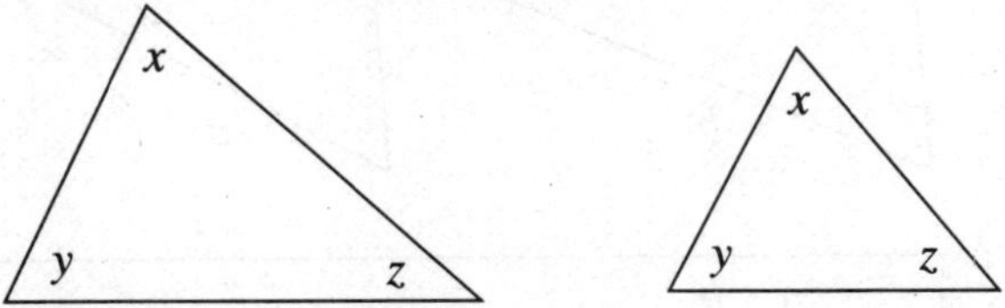

2 All corresponding sides are in equal proportion.

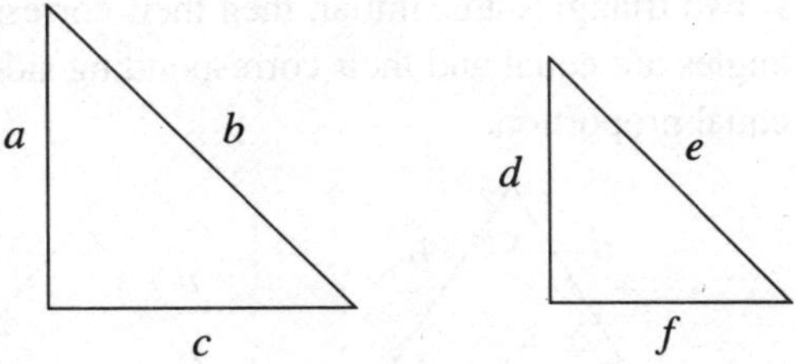

$$\frac{a}{d} = \frac{b}{e} = \frac{c}{f}$$

3 Two pairs of corresponding sides are in equal proportion and the included angle equal.

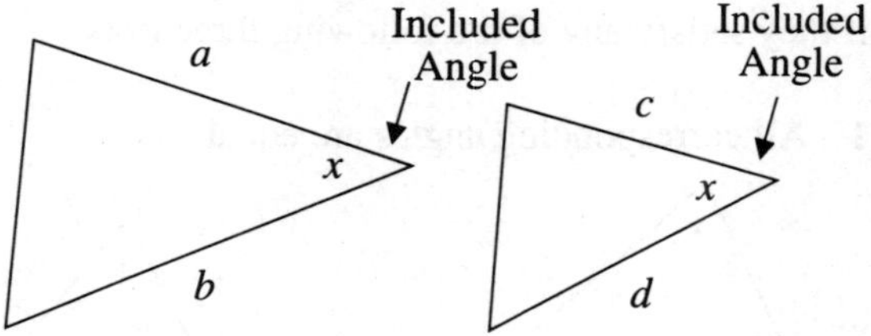

$$\frac{a}{c} = \frac{b}{d} \text{ and the included angle equal}$$

If two triangles are similar, then their corresponding angles are equal and their corresponding sides are in equal proportion.

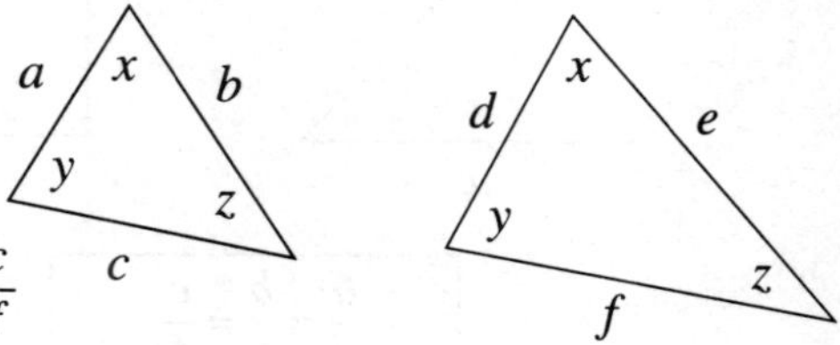

$$\frac{a}{d} = \frac{b}{e} = \frac{c}{f}$$

The symbol ||| means 'is similar to'.

D PROPERTIES OF QUADRILATERALS

QUADRILATERAL	PROPERTIES
Parallelogram	• opposite sides equal and parallel • opposite angles equal • diagonals bisect each other
Rhombus	• all properties of a parallelogram **plus** • diagonals bisect at right angles • diagonals bisect the angles through which they pass
Rectangle	• all properties of a parallelogram **plus** • diagonals are equal
Square	• all of the above properties

E ACCEPTABLE ABBREVIATIONS

In solving geometry questions, abbreviations should be used by students as a time-saving device, particularly in exams. Students are, however, strongly discouraged from inventing their own as it may lead to confusion and ultimately loss of marks.

Listed below is a comprehensive list of acceptable abbreviations commonly used in geometry.

MEANING	SYMBOL
angle	$\angle$
angles	$\angle$'s
parallel to	$\parallel$
perpendicular to	$\perp$
triangle	Δ
isosceles triangle	isos Δ
equilateral triangle	equil Δ
right angle	⦜
straight angles	st $\angle$'s
equal	=

MEANING	SYMBOL
quadrilateral	quad.
parallelogram	param.
vertically opposite	vert. opp.
alternate	alt.
co-interior	co-int.
complementary	comp.
supplementary	supp.

EXAMPLE 1

Find x in each of the following, giving reasons for your answer:

i

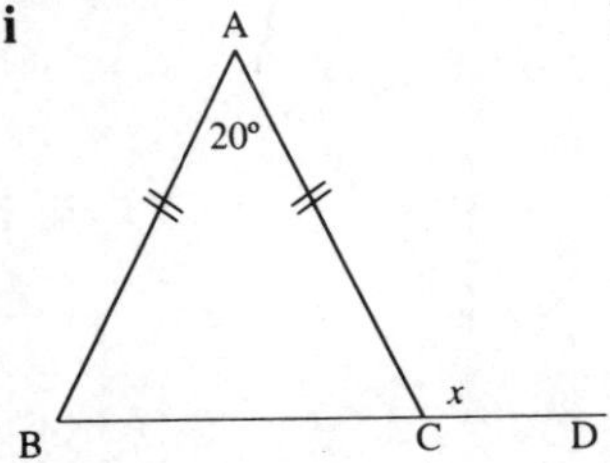

ii

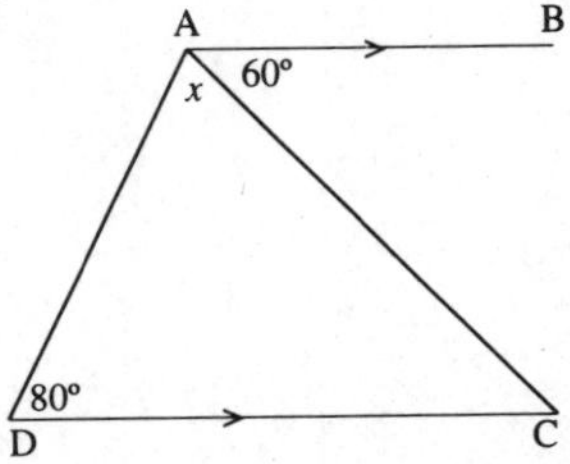

iii

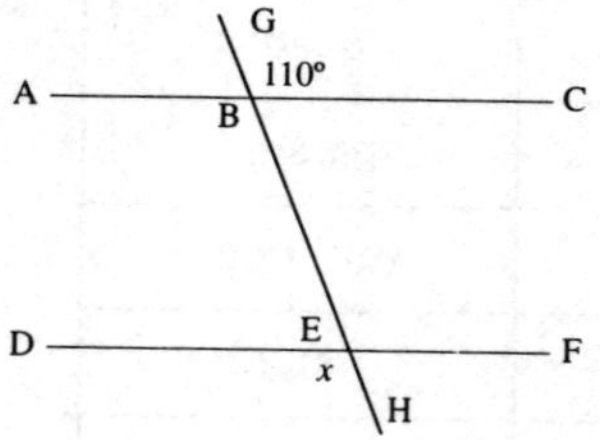

iv

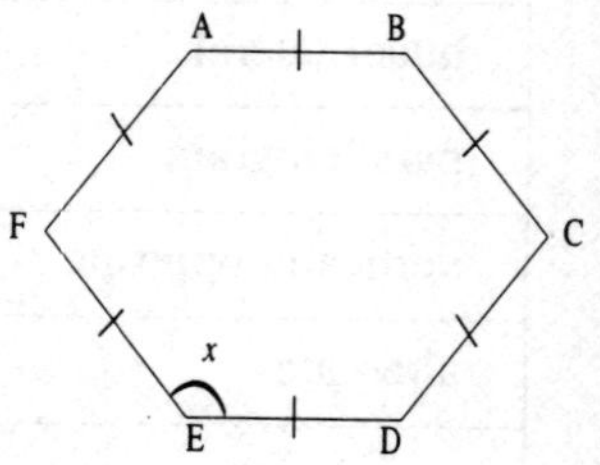

v

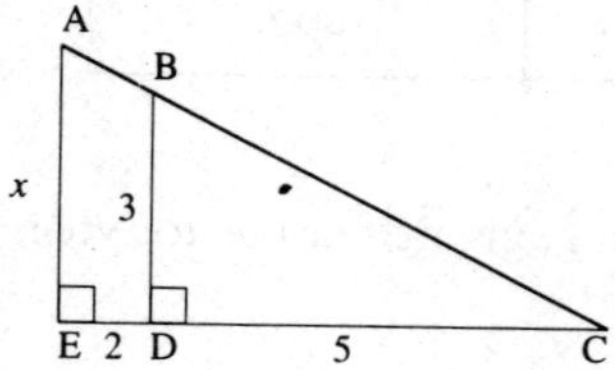

vi

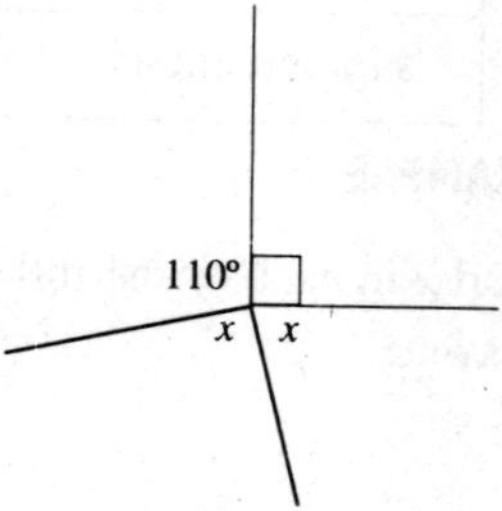

SOLUTION 1

i $\angle ACB = \angle ABC$ (base $\angle$'s of isos.Δ =)

$\angle ACB + \angle ABC = 160^\circ$ ($\angle$ sum of $\Delta = 180^\circ$)

$\therefore \angle ACB = 80^\circ$

$\therefore x = 180^\circ - 80^\circ$ (st. $\angle$'s sum to 180°)

$= 100^\circ$

ii $\angle BAD = \angle ADC$ (coint. $\angle$'s supp.)

$\therefore x + 60^\circ + 80^\circ = 180^\circ$

ie $x = 40^\circ$

iii $\angle FEB = 110^\circ$ (corresp. $\angle$'s =)

$\angle DEH = 110^\circ$ (vert. opp. $\angle$'s =)

iv $ABCDEF$ is a regular hexagon

sum of angles $= (2n - 4) \times 90^\circ$

$= (2 \times 6 - 4) \times 90^\circ$

$= 8 \times 90^\circ = 720^\circ$

$6x = 720^\circ$

$\therefore x = 120^\circ$

v $\angle BCD = \angle ACE$ (same $\angle$)

$\angle BDC = \angle AEC = 90^\circ$

$\therefore \Delta AEC \mathbin{|||} \Delta BDC$ (AAA)

Thus: $\dfrac{BD}{CD} = \dfrac{AE}{EC}$ (corresp. sides of ||| Δ's in = proportion)

$$\frac{3}{5} = \frac{x}{7}$$

$$\therefore x = \frac{21}{5} = 4.2 \text{ cm}$$

vi Angles meeting at a point sum to 360°

$$\therefore 2x + 110^\circ + 90^\circ = 360^\circ$$

$$2x = 160^\circ$$

$$x = 80^\circ$$

EXAMPLE 2

i Prove: $\Delta AED \mathbin{|||} \Delta BEC$

ii Hence find the length of *BC*.

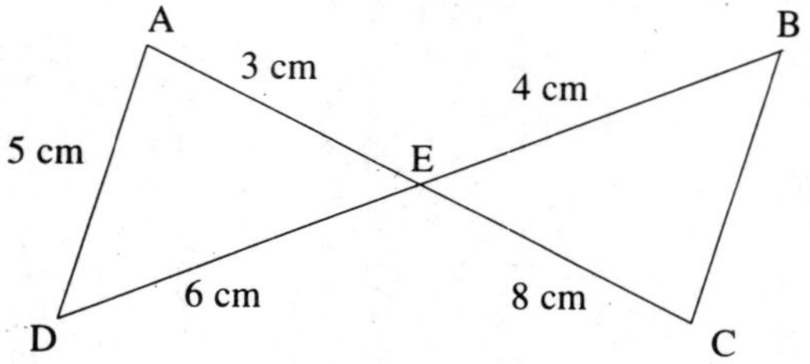

SOLUTION 2

i $\angle AED = \angle BEC$ (vert. opp. $\angle$s =)

$\frac{AE}{BE} = \frac{3}{4}$

$\frac{DE}{EC} = \frac{6}{8} = \frac{3}{4}$

ie $\frac{AE}{BE} = \frac{DE}{EC}$

$\therefore \Delta AED \ ||| \ \Delta BEC$

(2 corresp. sides in = proportion and the included $\angle$=)

ii $\frac{AD}{BC} = \frac{3}{4}$

ie $\frac{5}{BC} = \frac{3}{4}$

$\therefore BC = \frac{20}{3}$

$= 6\frac{2}{3}$ cm

A BASIC TRIGONOMETRIC RATIOS

$$\sin\theta = \frac{\text{opposite}}{\text{hypotenuse}} \quad \text{(SOH)}$$

$$\cos\theta = \frac{\text{adjacent}}{\text{hypotenuse}} \quad \text{(CAH)}$$

$$\tan\theta = \frac{\text{opposite}}{\text{adjacent}} \quad \text{(TOA)}$$

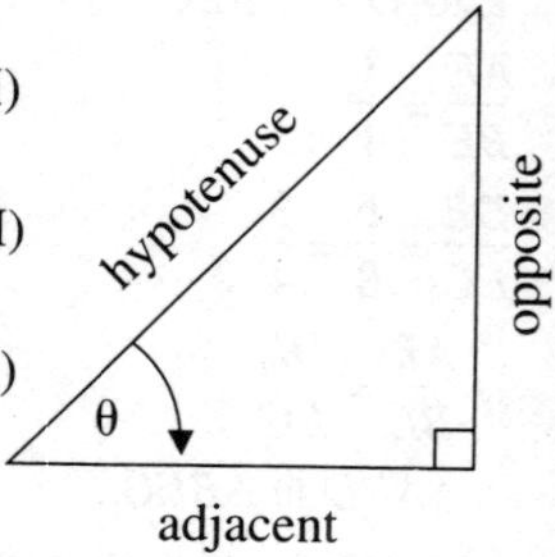

Hint: To help you remember the three ratios, here is a mnemonic:

S	**O**	**H**	**C**	**A**	**H**	**T**	**O**	**A**
h	n	e	r	f	e	r	v	l
a		n	y	t		i	e	i
m		r	i	e		p	r	c
e		y	n	r		p		e
			g			e		
						d		

EXAMPLE

Find the value of x in each of the following:

i

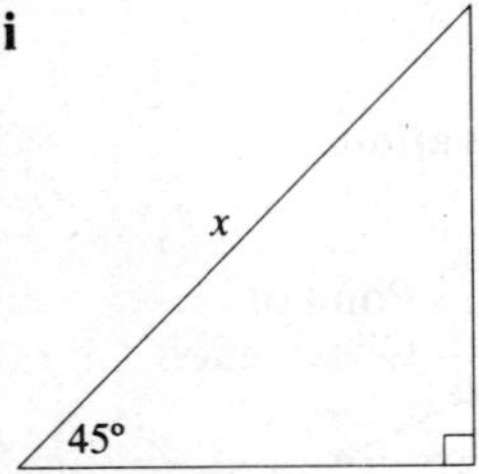

ii

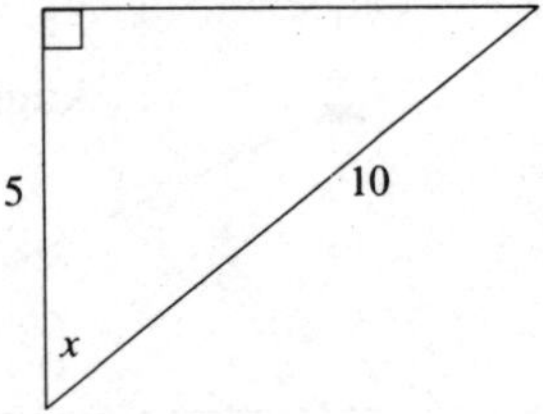

SOLUTION

i

$$\sin 45° = \frac{\text{opp.}}{\text{hyp.}} = \frac{12}{x}$$

$$\therefore x = \frac{12}{\sin 45°}$$

$$= 16.97 \text{ cm correct to 2 d.p.}$$

ii

$$\cos x = \frac{\text{adj.}}{\text{hyp.}} = \frac{5}{10} = \frac{1}{2}$$

$$\therefore x = \frac{12}{\sin 45°}$$

$$\therefore x = 60°$$

B ANGLES OF ELEVATION & DEPRESSION

Angles of elevation and depression are always measured **from the horizontal**. Refer to the diagrams below for details.

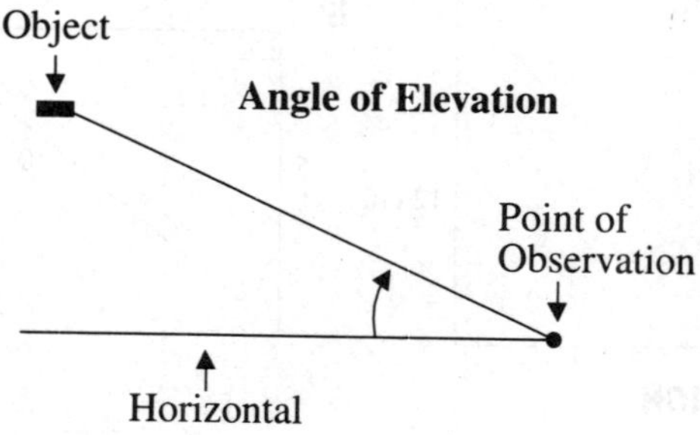

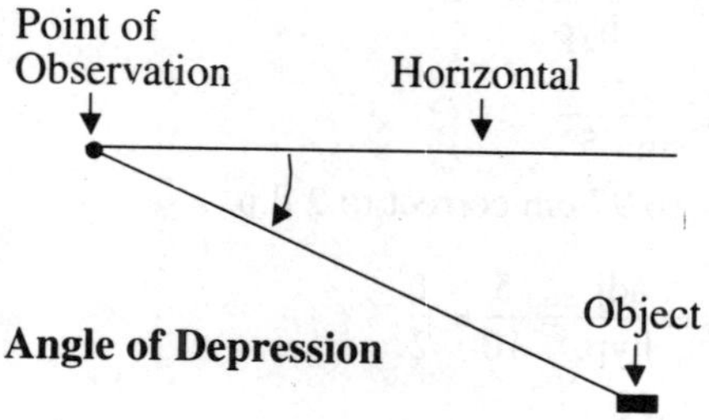

EXAMPLE 1

The angle of elevation of a tree from a point *A* 20 metres away is 42°15′. Calculate the height of the tree correct to two decimal places.

SOLUTION 1

Let the height of the tree = h

$$\tan 42°15' = \frac{h}{20}$$

$$\therefore h = 20 \tan 42°15'$$

$$= 18.17 \text{ m}$$

correct to 2 d.p.

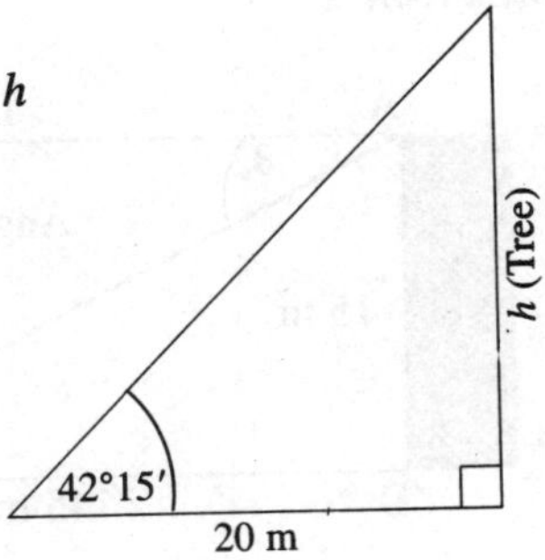

EXAMPLE 2

From the top of a building 15 m high, a woman observes a car located on ground level at a distance of 145 m from the base of the building. Find the angle of depression to the nearest minute.

SOLUTION 2

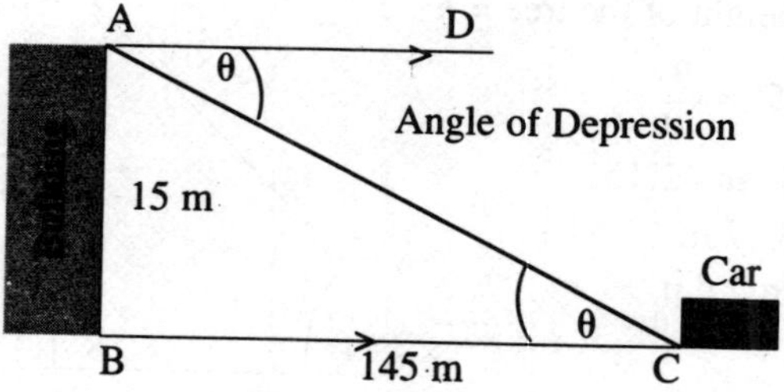

Let the angle of depression = θ

$\angle ACB = \theta$ (alt. $\angle$'s equal, $AD \parallel BC$)

$\therefore \tan\theta = \dfrac{\text{opp.}}{\text{hyp.}} = \dfrac{15}{145}$

$\therefore \theta = 5°54'$ to the nearest minute.

C THE SINE RULE

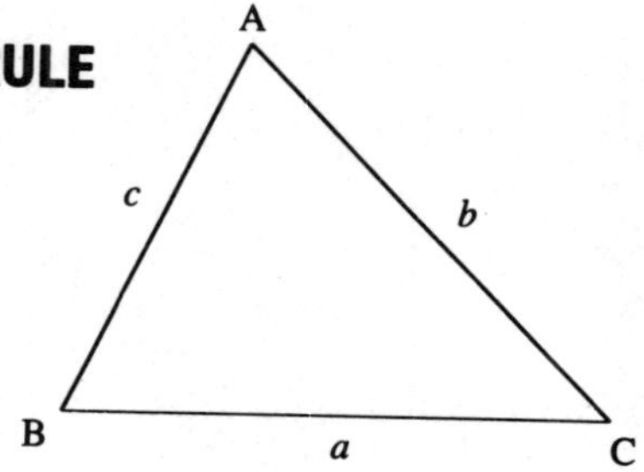

i Sine Rule

$$\frac{a}{\sin A} = \frac{b}{\sin B} = \frac{c}{\sin C}$$

Where a, b and c are the sides opposite the angles A, B and C.

The Sine rule is used to:

1. find the length of a side where 2 angles and 1 side are given.
2. find the size of an angle where 2 sides and 1 angle opposite one of the 2 sides is given.

ii Cosine Rule

$$a^2 = b^2 + c^2 - 2bc \cos A \quad \text{or}$$

$$\cos A = \frac{b^2 + c^2 - a^2}{2bc}$$

Where b and c are two given sides, A is the included angle and a is the remaining side.

The Cosine rule is used to:

1 find the length of a side where 2 sides and the included angle is given.

2 find the size of an angle where all 3 sides are given.

EXAMPLE 1

Using the sine rule, find the size of the acute angle $\angle ABC$ to the nearest degree.

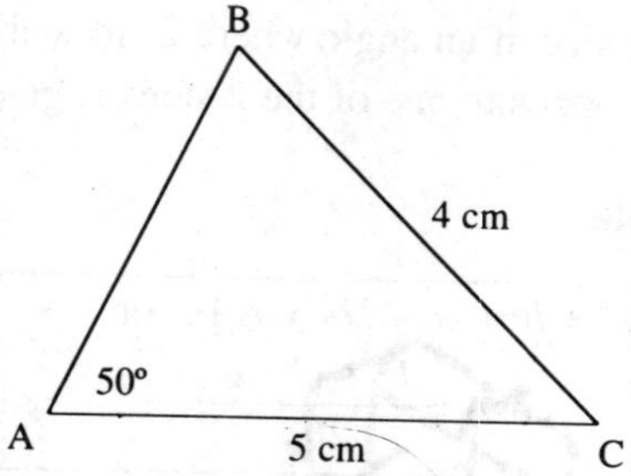

SOLUTION 1

$$\frac{a}{\sin A} = \frac{b}{\sin B}$$

ie $$\frac{4}{\sin 50^\circ} = \frac{5}{\sin B}$$

$$\therefore \sin B = \frac{5 \sin 50^\circ}{4} = 0.957$$

$$B = 73^\circ$$

ie $\angle ABC = 73^\circ$ to the nearest degree

EXAMPLE 2

Find using the cosine rule the length of AB correct to 1 decimal place.

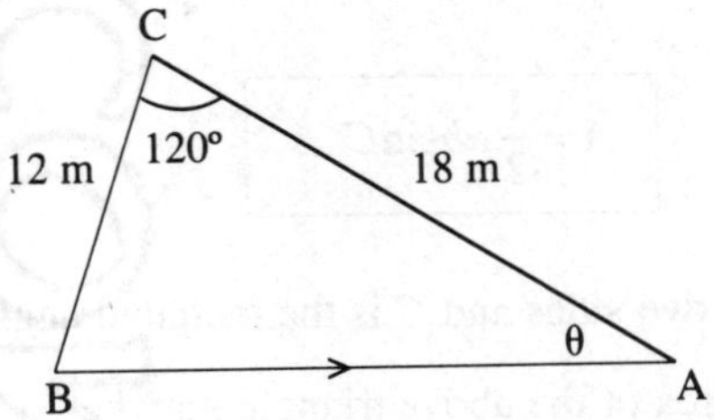

$$a^2 = b^2 + c^2 - 2bc \cos A$$

$$AB^2 = 12^2 + 18^2 - 2 \times 12 \times 18 \cos 120^\circ$$

$$= 468 - (-216)$$

$$= 684$$

$\therefore AB = 26.2$ m correct to 1 d.p.

D THE AREA OF A TRIANGLE

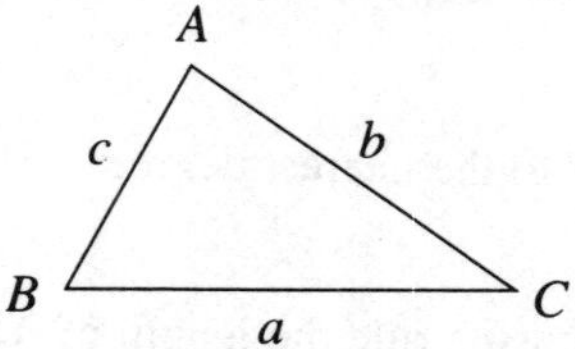

The area of any triangle can be found using the formula:

$$A = \frac{1}{2}ab\sin C$$

where a, b are two sides and C is the included angle.

Similarly the area of the above triangle may be expressed as:

$$A = \frac{1}{2}ac\sin B$$

$$A = \frac{1}{2}bc\sin A$$

EXAMPLE

Calculate the area of ΔOAB to the nearest whole number.

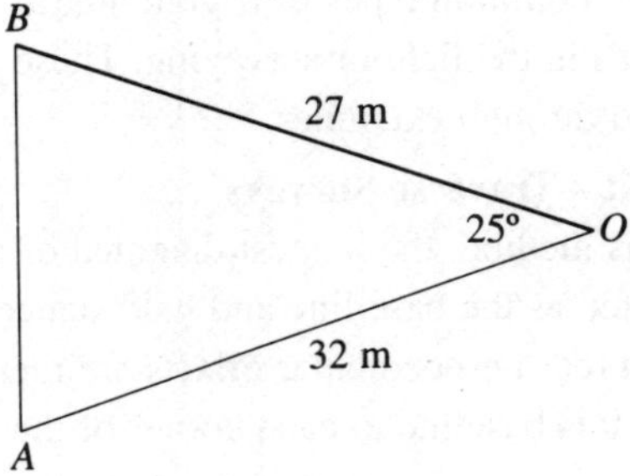

SOLUTION

$$\text{Area} = \frac{1}{2}ab \sin C$$

$$= \frac{1}{2}(OA)(OB) \sin C$$

$$= \frac{1}{2} \times 32 \times 27 \times \sin 25°$$

$$= 182.57$$

$$= 183 \text{ to the nearest whole number}$$

$\therefore$ The area of $\Delta OAB = 183 \text{ m}^2$.

E TRIGONOMETRIC APPLICATIONS – SURVEYING

There are 2 common types of trigonometric applications in the field of surveying. These are best understood through examples.

i **Offset – Traverse Surveys**

In this method, the longest diagonal of a field is selected as the base line and its distance is measured. Perpendicular offsets are then measured from this baseline to each corner of the field.

EXAMPLE

A surveyor's notebook is as follows:

	A	
	60	
	30	15
25	10	
	0	
	B	

Find the area of the field if all measurements are in metres.

SOLUTION

Area of the field $ABCD$

$= \text{area of } \Delta ABF + \text{area of } \Delta ABC$

$= \frac{1}{2} \times AB \times EF + \frac{1}{2} \times AB \times DC$

$= \frac{1}{2} \times 60 \times 25 + \frac{1}{2} \times 60 \times 15$

$= 750 + 450$

$= 1200 \text{ m}^2$

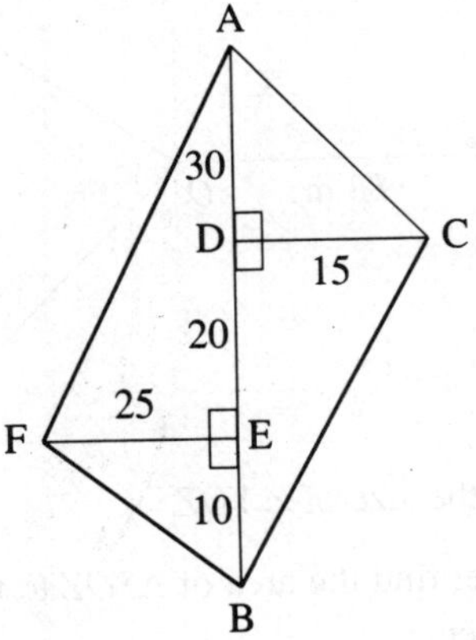

ii Radial Survey

With this method, the distances and compass bearings from a fixed point to the corners of a field are measured. The cosine rule is often required in answering these questions.

EXAMPLE

The diagram below shows the radial survey of a property.

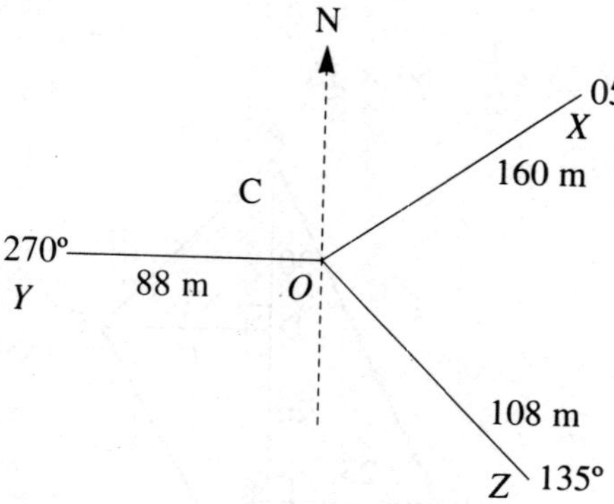

i Find the size of $\angle YOZ$.

ii Hence, find the area of ΔYOZ to the nearest whole number.

SOLUTION

i

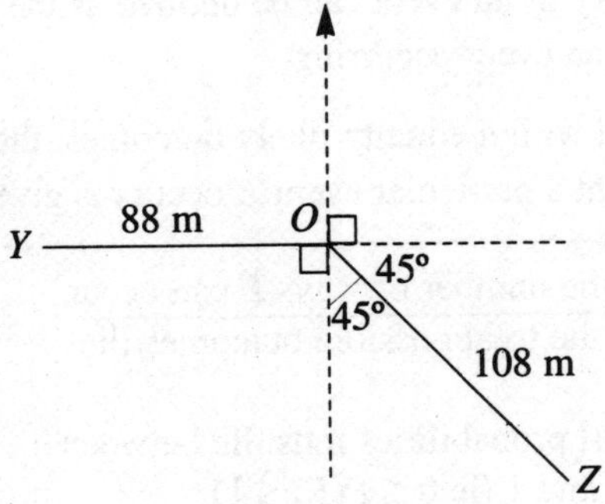

$\therefore \angle YOZ = 90° + 45° = 135°$

ii Area of $\Delta YOZ = \frac{1}{2}ab \sin C$

Area of $\Delta YOZ = \frac{1}{2} \times 88 \times 108 \times \sin 135°$

$= 3360.17...$

$= 3360 \text{ m}^2$

to the nearest whole number.

A THE PROBABILITY OF AN EVENT

The probability of an event can be defined as the likelihood of an event occurring.

Thus in a trial with n equally likely outcomes, the probability that a particular event E occurs is given by:

$$P(E) = \frac{\text{the number of ways } E \text{ can occur}}{\text{the total possible outcomes } (n)}$$

Note: All probabilities must lie between 0 and 1 (ie $0 \leq P(E) \leq 1$)

B THE PROBABILITY AN EVENT DOES NOT OCCUR

If $P(E)$ is the probability that event A occurs and $P(\bar{E})$ is the probability the event does not occur, then:

$$P(\bar{E}) = 1 - P(E)$$

EXAMPLE

A box contains 6 red, 5 green, 2 black and 1 white jellybeans. One jellybean is selected at random, find the probability that it is:

i red

ii black or white

iii not green

SOLUTION

i $P(\text{red}) = \dfrac{\text{total number of red jellybeans}}{\text{total number of jellybeans}}$

$P(\text{red}) = \dfrac{6}{14} = \dfrac{3}{7}$

ii $P(\text{black or white})$

$= \dfrac{\text{total number of black or white jellybeans}}{\text{total number of jellybeans}}$

$P(\text{black or white}) = \dfrac{3}{14}$

iii $P(\text{not green}) = 1 - P(\text{green})$

$= 1 - \dfrac{6}{14}$

$= \dfrac{8}{14} = \dfrac{4}{7}$

C TREE DIAGRAMS

Tree diagrams can be used in certain circumstances to calculate all possible outcomes of an experiment (ie to determine the sample space).

EXAMPLE

Anna tosses a coin twice.
Find the probability that she tosses:

i one head and one tail

ii two tails

SOLUTION

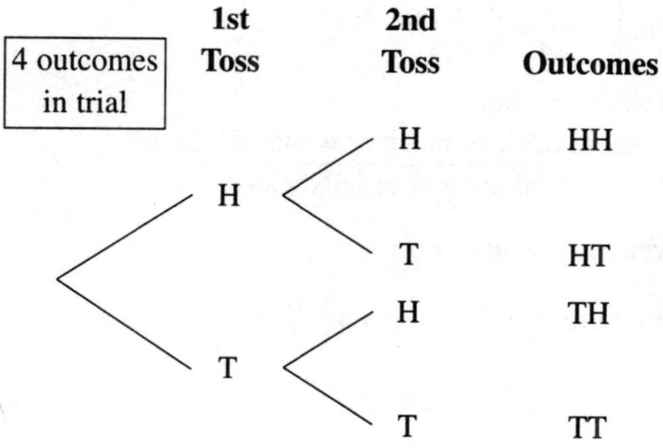

i $P(\text{HT}) = \frac{2}{4} = \frac{1}{2}$ **ii** $P(\text{TT}) = \frac{1}{4}$

D OTHER TECHNIQUES

There are a number of other techniques (apart from tree diagrams) that can be used to determine the sample space.

These techniques are basic but are often the most efficient method to answering the question. They include tables, lists or counting methods. A table is commonly the easiest way to answer questions involving dice.

EXAMPLE

Brett throws two dice. Find the probability that the sum on the uppermost faces is:

i greater than 8 **ii** less than 5

SOLUTION

Drawing up a table of all possible outcomes gives:

1, 1	**2, 1**	**3, 1**	4, 1	5, 1	6, 1
1, 2	**2, 2**	3, 2	4, 2	5, 2	6, 2
1, 3	2, 3	3, 3	4, 3	5, 3	6, 3*
1, 4	2, 4	3, 4	4, 4	5, 4*	6, 4*
1, 5	2, 5	3, 5	4, 5*	5, 5*	6, 5*
1, 6	2, 6	3, 6*	4, 6*	5, 6*	6, 6*

i $P(\text{greater than } 8) = \frac{10}{36}$

$= \frac{5}{18}$

(events indicated by *)

ii $P(\text{less than } 5) = \frac{6}{36} = \frac{1}{6}$

(events indicated in **bold**)

A SURDS

Numerical expressions that involve irrational numbers are called **surds**.

B RULES FOR SURDS

It is imperative that you are familiar with the following properties of surds as these will form the essential foundations for maths in Years 11 and 12.

1 $\sqrt{a} \times \sqrt{a} = a$

2 $\sqrt{a} \times \sqrt{b} = \sqrt{ab}$

3 $a\sqrt{b} + c\sqrt{b} = (a + c)\sqrt{b}$

4 $a\sqrt{b} \times c\sqrt{b} = ac\sqrt{b^2} = acb$

5 $\sqrt{a^2b} = \sqrt{a^2} \times \sqrt{b} = a\sqrt{b}$

Rationalising the Denominator

If the denominator of a fraction is irrational, we can rationalise the denominator by multiplying top and bottom by the same surd found in the denominator.

> If surd is in the form of $\frac{1}{\sqrt{a}} \times$ by $\frac{\sqrt{a}}{\sqrt{a}}$
>
> If surd is in the form of $\frac{\sqrt{b}}{\sqrt{a}} \times$ by $\frac{\sqrt{a}}{\sqrt{a}}$

EXAMPLES

Simplify the following:

i $2\sqrt{5} + \sqrt{125}$

ii $(2\sqrt{3})^2$

iii $\frac{\sqrt{6}}{\sqrt{2}}$

iv $\frac{\sqrt{5}}{\sqrt{3}}$

SOLUTION

Simplify the following:

i $2\sqrt{5} + \sqrt{125} = 2\sqrt{5} + \sqrt{25} \times \sqrt{5}$
$= 2\sqrt{5} + 5\sqrt{5} = 7\sqrt{5}$

ii $(2\sqrt{3})^2 = 2\sqrt{3} \times 2\sqrt{3}$
$= 2 \times 2 \times \sqrt{3} \times \sqrt{3} = 4 \times 3 = 12$

iii $\frac{\sqrt{6}}{\sqrt{2}} = \frac{\sqrt{3} \times \cancel{\sqrt{2}}}{\cancel{\sqrt{2}}} = \sqrt{3}$ **iv** $\frac{\sqrt{5}}{\sqrt{3}} = \frac{\sqrt{5} \times \sqrt{3}}{\sqrt{3} \times \sqrt{3}} = \frac{\sqrt{15}}{3}$

C INDEX LAWS

Index laws are vitally important as they are often required in simplifying algebraic expressions and solving equations. Students should make a determined effort to commit these laws to memory as they are a frequent source of difficulty for HSC students.

1 $x^0 = 1$	**2** $\sqrt[n]{x} = x^{\frac{1}{n}}$
3 $x^{-a} = \frac{1}{x^a}$	**4** $x^a \times x^b = x^{a+b}$
5 $\sqrt{x} = x^{\frac{1}{2}}$	**6** $\frac{x^a}{x^b} = x^{a-b}$
7 $(x^a)^b = x^{ab}$	**8** $(xy)^a = x^a \times y^a$

EXAMPLE

Simplify the following:

i $9^{\frac{1}{2}}$ **ii** $27^{\frac{1}{3}}$ **iii** 5^{-2}

iv $x\sqrt{x}$ **v** $(x\sqrt{x})^3$ **vi** $(x^4)^{\frac{5}{2}}$

SOLUTION

i $9^{\frac{1}{2}} = \sqrt{9} = 3$

ii $27^{\frac{1}{3}} = \sqrt[3]{27} = 3$

iii $5^{-2} = \frac{1}{5^2} = \frac{1}{25}$

iv $x\sqrt{x} = x \times \sqrt{x}$

$x\sqrt{x} = x^1 \times x^{\frac{1}{2}} = x^{1\frac{1}{2}} = x^{\frac{3}{2}}$

v $(x\sqrt{x})^3 = (x^{\frac{3}{2}})^3 = x^{\frac{9}{2}}$

vi $(x^4)^{\frac{5}{2}} = (\sqrt{x^4})^5$

$= (x^2)^5$

$= x^{2\times5}$

$= x^{10}$

D THE EXPONENTIAL $y = a^x$ and $y = a^{-x}$

i Graph of $y = 2^x$

x	-3	-2	-1	0	1	2	3
y	$\frac{1}{8}$	$\frac{1}{4}$	$\frac{1}{2}$	1	2	4	8

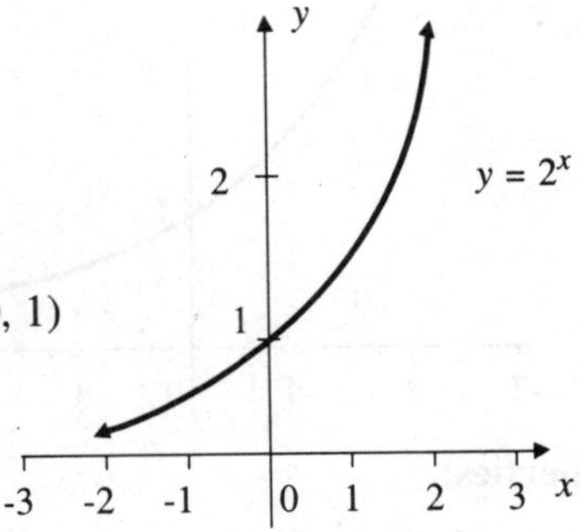

Properties:

- passes through (0, 1)
- always positive
- increases with increasing values of x.

Note: All exponential curves in the form $y = a^x$ where $a \geqslant 2$ resemble the above curve

ii Graph of $y = 2^{-x}$

x	– 3	– 2	– 1	0	1	2	3
y	8	4	2	1	½	¼	⅛

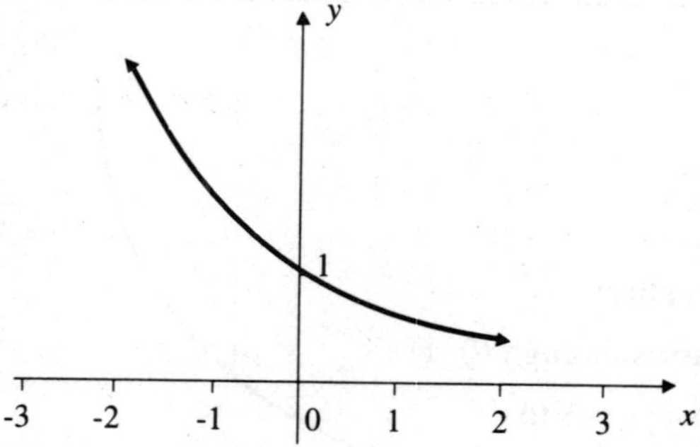

Properties:

- passes through (0, 1)
- always positive
- decreases with increasing values of x
  (ie approaches x-axis)

Note: All exponential curves in the form $y = a^{-x}$ where $a \geqslant 2$ resemble the above curve.

A QUADRATIC EXPANSIONS/ FACTORISATIONS

You need to be familiar with the following quadratic expansions/factorisations. Note that working backwards (ie right to left) is the factorisation process.

1 $(x + a)^2 = x^2 + 2ax + a^2$
2 $(x - a)^2 = x^2 - 2ax + a^2$
3 $(x + a)(x - a) = x^2 - a^2$
4 $(x + a)(x + b) = x^2 + (a + b)x + ab$

EXAMPLE 1

Expand the following and simplify:

i $(x + 1)(x - 5)$ **ii** $(x + 2)^2$

iii $(x + 5)^2 - (x - 5)^2$ **iv** $(2x - 3)^2$

SOLUTION 1

i $(x + 1)(x - 5) = x^2 - 5x + x - 5$
$= x^2 + (1 - 5)x - 5$
$= x^2 - 4x - 5$

ii $(x + 2)^2 = x^2 + 2(2)(x) + 2^2$
$= x^2 + 4x + 4$

iii $(x + 5)^2 - (x - 5)^2$
$= x^2 + 2(5)x + 5^2 - [x^2 - 2(5) + (5)^2]$
$= x^2 + 10x + 25 - (x^2 - 10x + 25)$
$= x^2 + 10x + 25 - x^2 + 10x - 25$
$= 20x$

iv $(2x - 3)^2 = (2x)^2 - 2(2x)(3) + (3)^2$
$= 4x^2 - 12x + 9$

EXAMPLE 2

Factorise the following:

i $4x - 40$ **ii** $2x^2 - 8$

iii $x^2 - 4x + 3$ **iv** $3x^2 + 7x + 2$

SOLUTION 2

i $4x - 40 = 4(x - 10)$

ii $2x^2 - 8 = 2(x^2 - 4)$

$= 2(x - 2)(x + 2)$

iii For $x^2 - 4x + 3$

$a + b = -4$

and $ab = 3$ (from equation 4)

$a = -3, b = -1$

$\therefore x^2 - 4x + 3 = (x - 3)(x - 1)$

iv For $3x^2 + 7x + 2$

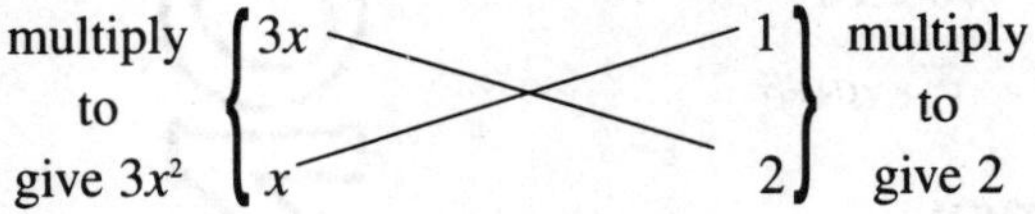

middle term

$6x + x = 7x$

$\therefore 3x^2 + 7x + 2 = (3x + 1)(x + 2)$

B GROUPING IN PAIRS

Four-term expressions are grouped in pairs and a common factor is taken from each pair.

$$\begin{aligned} ac + ad + bc + bd &= a(c + d) + b(c + d) \\ &= (a + b)(c + d) \end{aligned}$$

EXAMPLE

Factorise the following:

i $a^2 - ab + ca - cb$

ii $a^2 - b^2 + a + b$

SOLUTION

i $$\begin{aligned} a^2 - ab + ca - cb &= a(a - b) + c(a - b) \\ &= (a + c)(a - b) \end{aligned}$$

ii $$\begin{aligned} a^2 - b^2 + a + b &= (a - b)(a + b) + (a + b) \\ &= (a - b + 1)(a + b) \end{aligned}$$

C SOLVING QUADRATIC EQUATIONS

i Basic Principle

If $a \times b = 0$, then either $a = 0$ or $b = 0$ or both.

ii Quadratic Formula

The solution to the quadratic equation
$ax^2 + bx + c = 0$ is given by:

$$x = \frac{-b \pm \sqrt{b^2 - 4ac}}{2a}$$

Note: Students should always check if the quadratic equation can be factorised first before resorting to the quadratic formula.

EXAMPLES

Solve the following:

i $x^2 - 7x = 0$ **ii** $x^2 - 8x + 16 = 0$

iii $2x^2 + 8x + 6 = 0$ **iv** $x^2 - 4x + 1 = 0$

SOLUTIONS

i
$$x^2 - 7x = 0$$
$$x(x - 7) = 0$$
$$x = 0, 7$$

ii
$$x^2 - 8x + 16 = 0$$
$$(x - 4)(x - 4) = 0$$
$$x = 4$$

iii
$$2x^2 + 8x + 6 = 0$$
$$(2x + 2)(x + 3) = 0$$
$$\therefore 2x + 2 = 0 \text{ or } x + 3 = 0$$
$$x = -1 \qquad x = -3$$

iv $x^2 - 4x + 1 = 0$

Now, $x^2 - 4x + 1$ can't be factorised

∴ we need to solve the equation using the quadratic formula.

$$x = \frac{-b \pm \sqrt{b^2 - 4ac}}{2a}$$

$$= \frac{-(-4) \pm \sqrt{(-4)^2 - 4(1)(1)}}{2(1)}$$

$$= \frac{4 \pm \sqrt{16 - 4}}{2}$$

$$= \frac{4 \pm \sqrt{12}}{2}$$

$$= \frac{4 \pm 2\sqrt{3}}{2}$$

$$= \frac{2(2 \pm \sqrt{3})}{2}$$

$$= 2 \pm \sqrt{3}$$

D SIMULTANEOUS EQUATIONS

Solving simultaneous equations involves finding the values of x and y which satisfy both equations. They can be solved algebraically using two methods:

- the substitution method
- the elimination method

If you only want to learn one method then the elimination method is easier as it involves less complex algebra.

EXAMPLE

Solve the following simultaneous equation:

$x + 3y = 4$ and $4x + 8y = 28$

Method 1: Substitution Method

$$x + 3y = 4 \quad ...(1)$$
$$4x + 8y = 28 \quad ...(2)$$

From (1), make x the subject:

ie $x = 4 - 3y$

Substituting this into (2), gives:

$4(4 - 3y) + 8y = 28$

$16 - 12y + 8y = 28$

$16 - 4y = 28$

$-4y = 12$

$y = -3$

Now, substituting $y = -3$ into (1), gives:

$x + 3(-3) = 4$

$x - 9 = 4$

$x = 13$

Method 2: Elimination Method

$x + 3y = 4$ ...(1)

$4x + 8y = 28$ ...(2)

$4 \times (1)$, gives:

$4x + 12y = 16$ ...(3)

(3) – (2) gives:

$4y = -12$

$y = -3$

Substituting $y = -3$ into (1), gives:

$x + 3(-3) = 4$

$x - 9 = 4$

$x = 13$

Listed below is a summary of the formulae required in solving coordinate geometry questions.

A FORMS OF STRAIGHT-LINE EQUATIONS

There are 3 basic forms:

i Lines parallel to the coordinate axes

These are lines of the form:

- $x = a$ (vertical line parallel to x-axis)
- $y = b$ (horizontal line parallel to y-axis)

ii The gradient form

These are lines of the form:

$y = mx + b$

where m is the gradient and b is the y-intercept.

This form of the straight line equation can be used to find the gradient of a line given in general form (refer to (iii)).

iii The general form

These are lines expressed in the form:

$y = ax + by + c = 0$

where $a \geqslant 0$ and a, b and c are integers.

B THE GRADIENT FORMULA

The gradient m, of a line joining 2 points A (x_1, y_1) and B (x_2, y_2):

$$m = \frac{y_2 - y_1}{x_2 - x_1}$$

C THE POINT GRADIENT FORMULA

The equation of a line passing through a point $A\ (x_1, y_1)$ and gradient m:

$$(y - y_1) = m(x - x_1)$$

D THE TWO POINT FORMULA

The equation of a line passing through 2 points $A\ (x_1, y_1)$ and $B\ (x_2, y_2)$:

$$(y - y_1) = \frac{y_2 - y_1}{x_2 - x_1}(x - x_1)$$

Note: The above formula is not essential to learn as it reduces to the point gradient formula, which by most student standards is easier to use.

E THE DISTANCE FORMULA

The distance d, between two points $A\ (x_1, y_1)$ and $B\ (x_2, y_2)$:

$$d = \sqrt{(x_2 - x_1)^2 + (y_2 - y_1)^2}$$

F THE MIDPOINT FORMULA

The midpoint M, of the interval joining $A\ (x_1, y_1)$ and $B\ (x_2, y_2)$:

$$M(x, y) = \left(\frac{x_1 + x_2}{2}, \frac{y_1 + y_2}{2}\right)$$

G PARALLEL AND PERPENDICULAR LINES

- Two lines with gradients m_1 and m_2 respectively are parallel if $m_1 = m_2$.
- Two lines with gradients m_1 and m_2 respectively are perpendicular if

$$m_1 m_2 = -1 \quad \left(\text{or } m_2 = \frac{-1}{m_1}\right)$$

H THE CONDITION FOR A POINT TO LIE ON A LINE

A point lies on a line when the coordinates of the point satisfy the equation of the line (ie if you substitute the x-value of the point into the line it yields the y-value of the point).

I CONCURRENCE AND COLLINEARITY

- Three or more **points** lying on the same line are **collinear** points
- Three or more **lines** passing through the same point are **concurrent** lines.

J CURVE SKETCHING

In this course students are expected to sketch curves by setting up a table of values, plotting the points and then joining the points to form the curve.

Students also need to be familiar with the basic shape of the following important functions.

1 $y = ax^3$ (Cubic)

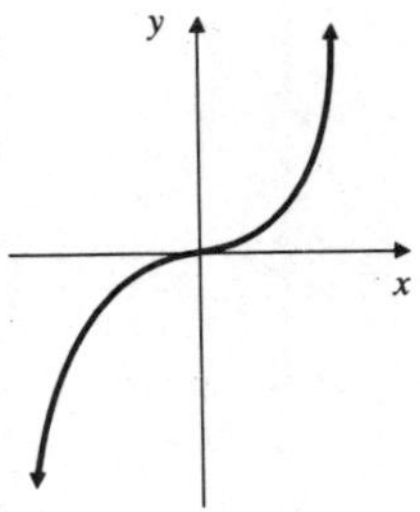

2 $y = -ax^3$ (Cubic)

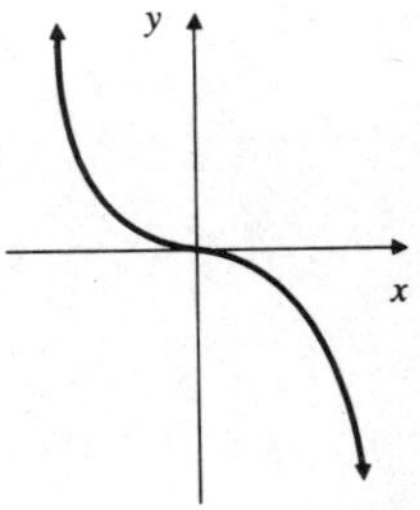

3 $y = ax^2$

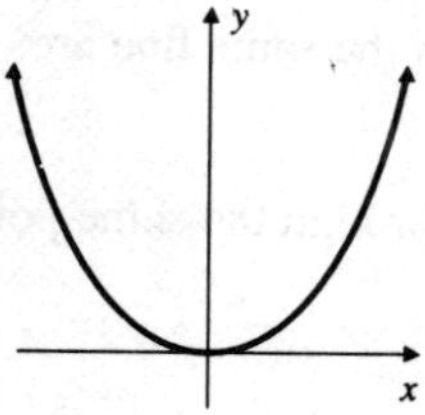

4 $y = -ax^2$

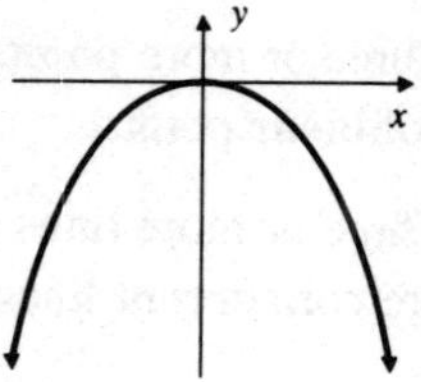

5 $y = ax^4$ (Quartic)

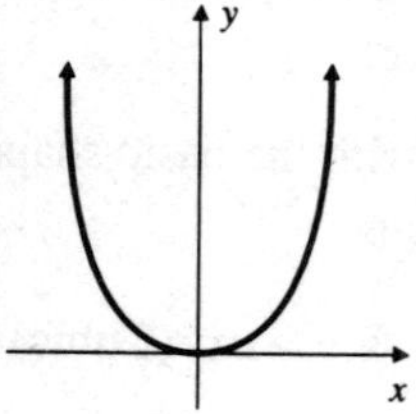

6 $y = -ax^4$ (Quartic)

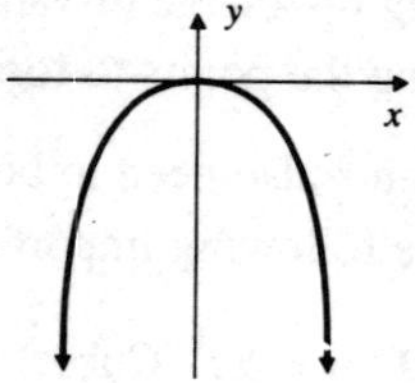